THINKING IN SYNC

A PRIMER ON THE MIND OF A MUSIC SUPERVISOR

AMANDA KRIEG THOMAS

Foreword by
PJ BLOOM

First edition April 2019

Cover Design by Traci Larson at Visual Issues

CONTENTS

ABOUT THE AUTHOR

Amanda Krieg Thomas has been working in the field of music supervision for over a decade. She started her career in music business affairs at Lionsgate, before moving over to the creative side in film and then television at the studio. She then explored the unscripted television world at Endemol Shine North America (formerly Reveille Studios) as a creative manager and music supervisor on shows such as *The Biggest Loser, MasterChef, One Born Every Minute* and *Rhett & Link: Commercial Kings*. From there Amanda was fortunate enough to obtain a position at Format Entertainment as music coordinator on several films including *Pitch Perfect 1* and *2, The Other Woman, Beyond The Lights*, and more, plus the ABC series, *Trophy Wife*, before transitioning to a music supervisor role at the company. As music supervisor she worked on several films including *American Girl: Grace Stirs Up Success* and the unscripted performance competition show *Fake Off*. In the summer of 2015 Amanda delved back into the television world, joining the stellar team at Neophonic, working on hit shows such as *The Americans, Pose, Claws, The Assassination of Gianni Versace: American Crime Story, Life In Pieces, American Horror Story, 9-1-1* and more. She remained at the company for three and a half years before launching her own endeavor, Yay Team Productions. Amanda is also a proud member of the Television Academy and on the Board of Directors for The Guild of Music Supervisors.

And along the way she has worked alongside many titans in the field. Needless to say she has plenty of experience receiving and responding to emails and music on behalf of herself and others.

...But really though, I'm just a music supervisor who is passionate about my work, the many different people I work with on a daily basis and using music to tell stories in the best way possible.

FOREWORD

BY PJ BLOOM

When I discovered film and television music in the early 1990s, it was my bolt-of-lightning career moment. I knew instantly it was to be my path. Like most of my peers, I stumbled upon the field accidentally. At that time no one went into this arena intentionally. You started on a more traditional music path - maybe creative, maybe administrative, maybe technical - then by some twist of fate you ended up here. But the moment I identified this world I knew instantaneously I had to be a part of it. And for nearly the entirety of my professional career I have dedicated my life to being a music supervisor and soundtrack executive. My work and commitment to the craft means more to me than I can ever express. I have benefited greatly both personally and professionally. I consider myself privileged to share the space with friends and colleagues whose contributions I hold dear. I am grateful to the filmmakers who provided me opportunity to hone my skills. And I am eternally grateful to have learned from the very best in the business.

Undoubtedly, one of the greatest early career perks of being a voracious scouter of music was access - access to everything and anything I could ever want in the space. As a buyer in a world of sellers, I could proactively request music from any source at any time then, almost magically, it would appear. As I built my career and worked on more and more relevant productions, music just showed up. It came by mail, by messenger, digitally - I even had a guy hand me his CD while I was in the barber's chair getting a haircut. In many ways this truth defined my personal bar for initial success. I wasn't making much money, but I didn't have to pay for music anymore. Heck, I barely had to ask for it. It just came. And that was beautiful!

Then something shifted... The music kept showing up. More and more of it - uncontrollably. It came from origins known and unknown. The same music appeared from multiple sources. Emails, CD's, vinyl, box sets - all commandeering precious office space and appropriating my inbox like a virus. It was unstoppable! Clearly no one cared what music I might want or need for my work. The simple perception that I was able to provide opportunity was enough for anyone who had music to share and could locate me. It was becoming unmanageable.

But this was only one issue. The more I delved into the deluge, it became frighteningly obvious that very few ever considered the notion that those assets needed to be cleared and licensed - in full, swiftly and without issue. I've now come to believe that most music purveyors have little understanding for what song clearance is nor any appreciation for the symbiosis between music creation, music peddling and the procurement of the very thing that drives this entire field.

I don't make this claim lightly. I do so from decades of experience; from witnessing my daily opportunity to be creative and provide the breadth of services for which I've been hired become overrun by the administrative quagmire of actually licensing the music folks work so hard to put in my hands. In my time as a music supervisor I've met many, many peers who feel the same way. The thrill of having a world of music at your fingertips has been replaced with suspicion and the exhaustion of legally using it. But all said, I also know it doesn't have to be this way. Music discovery can still be beautiful!

I have had the pleasure of working closely with Amanda Krieg Thomas for years. I have taught her and I have learned from her. Amanda shares my passion to preserve the integrity of this field. She does so selflessly and with grace in the hopes the knowledge she shares will help others create a culture of awareness, opportunity and ultimate success. *Thinking In Sync* is a unique perspective written by an industry insider who spends every day on the frontline. This book will educate. It may frustrate. But the hope is it provides a foundation that breeds stronger business practices and inspires anyone who reads it to try harder and reach higher.

INTRODUCTION

"How do I get you my music?"

"What is your submission policy?"

"What are you working on?"

Music supervisors, a very small group of music buyers in a big world of music sellers, are asked these questions (and others) every moment of every day. In meetings, over email, in person, via social networking, during lunch (and breakfast and dinner) – no matter where we are or what we are doing we encounter music creators and content providers interested in getting their music placed in film and television.

It's not a surprise why, of course. We completely understand where such questions are coming from. The problem is that the answers – as in, answers that will actually get an artist further towards the goal of getting songs placed in media - are much more complex than you'd think. There is so much more to achieving that goal than simply sending the music.

If you have years of experience pitching songs and collaborating with music supervisors then you've probably already mastered your own tested strategies for music submissions, checking in, responding to specific song requests (a/k/a "music searches" or "creative briefs") and more over time. This book might not be for you...though it's certainly possible you'll gain fresh insight into current trends and new preferences you weren't aware of before.

No, it is those new to the game that ask these questions:

- Recording artists, songwriters (or their managers) interested in exploring sync opportunities and unsure where to start
- Passionate music lovers who have been asked to help represent the music of friends, or who have just amassed enough tracks and want to start their own catalog.
- Individuals just starting out in the music industry who have landed a job requiring interaction with music supervisors for the first time.

If you fall into any of the above categories, then you're in the right place.

This book will aim to provide the most comprehensive answer to "How do I get you my music" as possible. I will cover creative approaches to consider during the songwriting process, a checklist for preparing the audio files in your catalog, best practices for reaching out to music supervisors, submission formats, and how to really get on the "music search list" and stay there (it is rarely by asking). I will not be exploring the intricacies of music publishing or copyright law, instead providing a basic overview of a few music publishing scenarios as they most frequently pertain to licensing music to music supervisors.

Before continuing however, it should be noted that there are no guarantees. Following the advice to come will not definitively result in your song being used in a television show or film (also called "placements" or "syncs" in the music licensing world). The chapters are not filled with precise strategies, case studies and proven methods for getting your music into media. Why not?

First off, I am speaking from only one perspective – that of a music supervisor, hired by Studios, Directors, Producers, Agencies, etc. to oversee the music needs for a project. A more comprehensive definition of the role will be provided shortly; the bottom line is that I do not represent or "pitch" a catalog of songs myself. It is very possible that peers who are well versed in this arena ("on the other side" as we sometimes say) will have differing experience and opinions, though several of such colleagues were consulted on the information that follows.

More importantly however there are no proven, fail-safe methods for getting placements, certainly none that can be put into a succinct checklist. Music needs are too elusive and ever changing and it's almost impossible to know for sure who is looking for what and when. Landing a placement can be as ephemeral as catching someone in a good mood, or being the one email they open that day because they happen to notice the band was from their hometown.

There are, however, some common tips and recommendations - and complaints - I've heard over and over again from fellow music supervisors in conversations and over many, many panels. This book is focused only on these absolute basics - a jumping off point to get you thinking "in synch." From here, I encourage you to gather more information, check out the resources mentioned throughout the book, attend conferences, dig deeper and continue honing your skills and knowledge. One word you will see often throughout this book is "research." The information that follows is merely the start of your research journey!

But where to even begin?

Having great music is an essential starting point, but what truly separates those we seek to do business with regularly are those who "get it" vs. those who don't. In order to fully understand how best to approach a music supervisor with your music, it's essential to understand the role of and demands on a music supervisor. The more you are willing and able to adapt to the Music Supervision process, the needs, stresses, concerns and vision behind it, the more likely you will be integrated into it.

With that said, the Guild of Music Supervisors defines the role of a music supervisor as:

A qualified professional who oversees all music related aspects of film, television, advertising, video games and any other existing or emerging visual media platforms as required. In addition:

1. The music supervisor must possess a comprehensive knowledge of how music impacts the visual medium. The music supervisor works with the key decision makers and/or designated creative team to collectively determine the musical vision, tone and style that best suits the project.

2. The music supervisor provides professional quality service that combines creative, technical and management expertise with relevant proven experience. This specialized combination of diversified knowledge and unique skills is integrated into all stages of development, pre-production, production, post-production, delivery and strategic marketing of the project with regard to all music related elements.

Music Supervisor Responsibilities include but are not limited to:

1. Identify, secure and supervise any and all music related talent, which includes composers,

songwriters, recording artists, on-camera performers, musicians, orchestrators, arrangers, copyists, contractors, music producers, engineers, etc.: liaise and negotiate with talent representation, including legal, label, talent management, agency, business management, etc.

2. Liaise and effectively communicate with other related and involved professionals & support staff, i.e. directorial, production, editorial, sound (production & post), camera, choreography, studio & network executives, advertising agencies, clients, label executives, game designers, distributors and cross-promotional marketing partners.

3. Possess an accurate knowledge of all costs associated with delivery of music elements. Determine and advise on financial needs of project and generate realistic budget with respect to all music related costs. Deliver all required music elements within the established budgetary parameters.

4. Advise on feasibility of schedule based on release, broadcast, campaign or product delivery. Deliver all music elements consistent with specific technical requirements. Manage and/or secure legal rights of new and existing recordings, clearances of Synchronization and Master use

licenses of pre-existing music, credits, cue sheets, etc. within scheduling parameters.

5. Determine the viability of, creation of and securing exposure or distribution of any music related ancillary product, i.e. soundtrack, single, video, internet downloads, etc. for the purpose of promotion or additional revenue streams.

_____

As you can see, there is much more to being a music supervisor than picking songs for scenes! Don't worry, this is not a book about music supervision. I do believe, however, that awareness and knowledge of certain aspects of the job will help you be more effective in *your* job. While this book may only dig deep in one or two of the areas described above, the rest should be used as a lens through which to understand how music supervisors work and why we respond the way we do.

1 ANATOMY OF A PLACEMENT

As mentioned, learning certain aspects of a music supervisor's job is critical to understanding all the information that follows. This chapter will describe key terms like "master recording" and "publishing", the functions of performance rights organizations, the director-music supervisor relationship, the clearance and licensing process from quote requests to licenses, music cue sheets, and more.

For the purposes of this book and as the role specifically relates to music sent to us, I believe the lynchpin of music supervision is song clearance. Music supervisors are skilled in many more areas of course; the description included in the introduction should provide some indication. It is the knowledge of and experience in song clearance, however, that truly separates a music supervisor from a song curator. In fact, the clearance process is so important - and at times so challenging, nuanced and time-consuming - that music clearance is its own profession. At the end of the day, if a song can't be cleared, it can't be used, and it's on to the next option.

As an artist, label, manager, agent or pitching company you'll want to do everything in your power to ensure your songs can be cleared easily. A snag or complication in the clearance process is often the fastest way to get thrown onto a music supervisor's "black list" (a dramatic, but unofficial term). With that in mind it is essential to understand the building blocks, needs and expectations of the this process, because doing as such will make you a music supervisor's best friend.

THE SONG CLEARANCE PROCESS

What does it mean for a song to be "cleared" (i.e. able to be used in media)? There are several different types of rights that pertain to the use of music in various scenarios.

Mechanical Rights – These rights grant the ability to reproduce a song for sale on a phonorecord (CD, vinyl, digital download, interactive stream) both for it's original release and outside of it, such as on a soundtrack or compilation album.

Public Performance Rights – These rights grant the ability to perform music for a public audience e.g. TV, movie theater, in a bar, in a restaurant, concert venue, on a plane or bus, etc. In the case of television in the United States, the television networks pay large one-time annual blanket fees to the Performance Rights Organizations (more on these shortly, but in the United States these are ASCAP, BMI, SESAC and GMR) for the right to perform songs publicly in their programming. The networks are then required to submit air date schedules of all the programs that are broadcast on their channels throughout the year, as well as music cue sheets (more on these later as well) that detail the use of all of the music used in their programming (e.g. background score, licensed songs, on air performances, etc.) The Performance Rights Organizations then use these cue sheets to identify the songwriters and music publishers and how much money in royalties they need to them pay out for the use of their music.

Synchronization Rights – These are the rights primarily discussed in this chapter and throughout the book. Synchronization rights are the rights required to place or reproduce – i.e. "synchronize" – music to picture in media. To be clear, granting the right to synchronize your song in media does not give the licensee (the film, television show, etc.) any ownership of the underlying copyright, only the right to use your copyright in their media.

As we begin our journey into the process of obtaining synchronization rights, it's important to understand the concept that any song you piece of music you hear on the radio can be broken into two parts: the **master recording** and the **composition**. And when it comes to clearing the rights to a composition, this is typically referred to as clearing the "publishing."

In brief, the master recording is the recorded performance created of a composition. The composition is the music itself – the lyrics (f any), the melody, chord progression, the notes on a page of sheet music, etc.

One or more parties can own, control, represent or administer both publishing and the master recording. The technical verbiage can depend on the type of deals done and with whom, but for the purposes of this book "own" or "control" will be used as encompassing terms. You're more likely to find multiple owners of the publishing than of master recordings, especially if there are several songwriters. To be able to use (or "synchronize") an existing recording in any media, all parties that control the master recording and publishing rights must grant synchronization rights to use the song in the picture - only then is a song considered "cleared" for use. If the party (whether a single person or company) that controls 2% of the publishing on a song does not grant synchronization rights, then the song is not cleared and cannot be used.

In music supervisor and Music Clearance lingo these two halves (the master recording and the publishing) are each considered one "side" of a song. To use this in context:

The fee for "Party Time" by The Clowns will be $2K a side.

This means the master recording will cost $2K to license, and the publishing will also cost $2K to license. The total cost to license the song will be $4K.

Or, the fee for "Party Time" by The Clowns will be $4K all in.

The costs are still the same as in the previous example; the term "all in" is used to refer to the total fee for the song, master recording and publishing combined.

Alright, I realize I went through that quickly. Let's break it down even further...

Master Recording Rights

These rights pertain to the master recording, i.e. the actual recorded expression of a song, which could be on CD, vinyl, digital download, etc. In order to use a master recording in a montage in a film, for example, an editor must take an actual audio file of the recording, put it into their editing software and merge it with the picture. The rights to use (or "synchronize") that recording are the master recording rights. Typically a record label controls the rights to the Master Recording – though it could be the recording artist themselves depending on the circumstance. Sometimes artists will record new versions of greatest hits and release them directly or on smaller labels years later after they are no longer signed to their original label.

If a band is performing on a television show or in a movie then master rights aren't required since no previously existing recording is being used (though permission might still need to be granted by the label.)

Note: The examples below are used only to illustrate the definition of a master recording. They should not be used for song clearance purposes.

Example 1

Song: "Get Lucky"

Daft Punk Version:
Master Recording is owned by Columbia Records (owned by Sony Music)
Publishing is owned by Sony/ATV Music Publishing and Imagem

Halestorm Version:
Master Recording is owned by Atlantic Records
Publishing is owned by Sony/ATV Music Publishing and Imagem

Example 2

Song: "What The World Needs Now Is Love"

Merrilee Rush Version:
Master Recording is owned by Sony Music
Publishing is owned by BMG

Dionne Warwick Version:
Master Recording is owned by Warner Music Group
Publishing is owned by BMG

While the master recording rights to a particular recording are owned and controlled by the recordings artist's label (or the artist directly, if there is no label), the owner of the publishing rights to the song itself will be with the same company regardless of the recording used.

Songwriting Shares

Songwriting shares represent the songwriter's contribution to the song and are tied to the publishing rights, i.e. each writer's share is represented by one or more of the publishers of the song. Songwriter shares are not cleared separately for use in media as the publishers are granting the rights to use the song on their behalf. However, for any given song, the songwriter shares must add up to 100% exactly. The breakdown of these shares is commonly referred to as writer "splits." If a music supervisor requests the "writer splits" for a song, they are asking for how these shares are divided (e.g. Bobby Ray has 25%, Jim Smith has 50% and Joe Thomas has 25%). Royalties are attributed to songwriter's shares when music is publicly performed (this includes music playing at restaurants and nightclubs and any public venue where music is played - live or recorded) and when any record is sold (in any format) so it's important to get this settled, so you or your clients can get paid.

By law, if there are two songwriters on a song the writer splits are considered to be 50% and 50% (or if there are three writers into thirds and so on), however that is not always the case. Writers can agree to any split (keep in mind this must add up to 100%), and this split is normally commensurate with each writer's contribution to the whole – though again, this is not always the case. Once there are more than three writers involved in a given composition, the breakdown of writer splits can get complicated.

Example 1

The Gingers: A four-person band with all equal partners that list each member as a songwriter per song with 25% share each.

Example 2

Johnny Red Tooth and the Rats: Johnny writes all of the lyrics and sings but gets some help from the four-member backing band on the music. He takes 50% for each song and the four backers split the remaining 50% at 12.5% each.

Publishing Rights

These rights are owned and/or controlled by those who control the song itself, i.e. the music and lyrics or the "copyright." This can be a so-called "major publisher" such as BMG, Sony/ATV Music Publishing, Warner/Chappell Music Publishing or Universal Music Publishing Group, a smaller "indie publisher" or simply the writers of the song themselves. Like songwriters, publishers also get paid performance royalties from Performance Rights Organizations.

If a writer hasn't assigned his or her rights to a third party publisher (more on those later) then by default that writer is also the publisher. As you see above, when there are multiple writers some decisions need to be made as to who gets what. As with songwriter shares, publisher shares need to add up to 100% as well, and the breakdown of these ownership percentages is commonly referred to as publishing "splits." If a music supervisor requests the "publishing splits" on a song they are asking for how the publishing rights are divided (e.g. Warner/Chappell Music Publishing controls 30%, Indie Music Publishing LLC controls 20% and Universal Music Publishing controls 50%). This information is essential for song clearance (unlike songwriters splits, though those can be very helpful for music supervisors in the research process).

A couple examples of various publishing split arrangements...

Example 1
The Gingers: A four-member band with all equal partners that list each member as a songwriter per song with 25% share each, **and each get an equal publishing share of 25% each**.

Example 2
They all agree that Johnny should take 50% of the songwriting rights, and the four other members split the remaining 50% at 12.5% each. However, since Johnny is the front man, primary songwriter, and handles all the

business for the band, **the four other members assign 100% of their publishing rights to Johnny** via a publishing deal or administration deal.

Such deals will be explored further later in the book, but the key takeaway is that if a Music Supervisor approaches Johnny about using one of the band's songs in a film, he has the right (and ability) to approve 100% of the publishing rights. If such an agreement is not in place, a Music Supervisor will need to approach Johnny and each of the band members individually to ask them to approve the use.

If you are already a registered ASCAP songwriter, you might be used to seeing a 50% split system between songwriter and publishing rights, rather than 100% as described above (which BMI and SESAC use). Always double-check that 100% of the songwriting rights and 100% of the publishing rights are accounted for when reviewing your ASCAP royalty statements or registering a song into the database. If you're not "registered" yet, don't worry — an explanation will be provided shortly.

Suffice to say, if you are in a band trying to get your music placed or are working on behalf of a band, *ownership needs to be decided upon as soon as possible and ideally prior to pitching music*, regardless of whether you have been set up by your manager to "co-write" with a stranger or are jamming with friends.

This applies to the master recording as well. As mentioned earlier, if there is a label involved, deciding master ownership is easier: presumably the label helped pay for recording and/or distribution, so they will own the master. These days though it can get fuzzy when it comes to indie music. Maybe the producer donated weeks of their time to work on the record, maybe the artist paid to record the album, but an indie "vinyl only" label is distributing it. Regardless of the arrangement, as an artist or songwriter it's always good to get this conversation out of the way early.

Along the same lines, it is wise to get clarity on who is able to approve clearance requests and sign off on licenses early on as well. For example, if the master recording is owned and controlled by the label, do you (the artist) want approval over all licenses? Or can they make those decisions without you? Do they need to consult you if they want to sign an overall administration or publishing deal with another company wherein that company will then be able to license your music? Can one writer sign off on licenses on behalf of all the writers (i.e. administer) as described in Example 2 above? It may seem a silly thing to confirm ("Well of course they would consult us on x, y or z") but I have seen such assumptions play out in a bad way. The bottom line: The bottom line: if you're going to successfully license your music, you need to sort out who controls and has the right to license the publishing and the master recording – be this one person or entity or several. If you play bass in a band but did not participate at all in the writing process, you are most likely not authorized to tell your girlfriend she can use it in her independent film.

Who on a Production initiates song clearance?

Often times it is the Music Supervisor, but many Music Supervisors will hire companies and people that specialize in music clearance (such as Jill Meyers, Meryl Ginsburg, Joey Singer, Christine Bergren, EMG and more) or have a studio music clearance department at their disposal, depending on the project. On really indie films where there is no music supervisor and almost no budget, sometimes the director or a producer will clear the music.

When in the process should a song be cleared?

A common misconception, among filmmakers especially, is that clearing a song obligates one to use it. They often wait until a film is almost done to even start the process. This can quickly turn into a disaster when they find out they cannot use a key song days before finishing.

Music supervisors will generally go out for clearance when a first choice, or few top song choices, have emerged. Ideally this process begins as early as possible, in the event the fee quoted is cost prohibitive or one of the parties denies the use and a replacement must be found. In such situations more time is always better.

If you as an artist receive a request from someone on a production (whether music supervisor or clearance company) to clear your song, asking for a quote (i.e. fee for the use), this is certainly a positive sign, but by no means a guarantee your song will get used.

Tracking down the right people

I cannot reiterate this enough: if a song can't be cleared, it can't be used. Once a song is in strong consideration for a scene the first step in the clearance process is tracking down the master owner and publisher(s).

In the best-case scenario, a music supervisor has submitted the song for consideration and has all of the relevant information on hand already. However with the proliferation of download sources from all across the Internet and so many cooks in the kitchen from editors to music editors and even writers' assistants, it can be impossible to control what audio file winds up in the cut prior to this information being tracked down.

Finding the owner of the master recording is usually straightforward, given recordings are typically owned by a single record label or recording artist. The label can often be identified through allmusic.com, iTunes or Amazon. Notice how I never say always - because there are always exceptions! This is followed by tracking down a contact at said label using the label or artist's website. While newer artists and labels frequently (though not always) have their information available, with older or defunct labels there is much more detective work involved. From there it's essential to ensure we are clearing the correct recording of the song being used, whether it is an original, extended version, re-master, re-record, live version, etc. which can be especially challenging when the audio is ripped from YouTube (as the case may be).

The publishing information has the potential to be much trickier given how many parties can be involved and the way songwriters' publishing catalogs can be bought, sold and divvied up by territory. First stops on the research train are the websites of the Performance Rights Organizations.

A quick detour on performance rights organizations.

This book aims to provide a brief overview and some context on how music supervisors specifically utilize and interact with these organizations. However, they serve a range of purposes beyond those described here. I recommend checking out their individual websites, as well as the article "What Is SoundExchange, ASCAP, BMI, PROs, HFA and How To Get All Your Royalties" by Ari Herstand on his Ari's Take blog for more in depth information.

Performance Rights Organizations (a/k/a "PROs") – PROs are organizations acting on behalf of songwriters and music publishers that grant public performance rights (as described earlier) to broadcasters and then pay royalties to songwriters and publishers for the public performance of their works. The U.S. has four such organizations - ASCAP, BMI, SESAC and GMR (membership in the last two being invite only) - that will collect and pay out performance royalties from around the world.

The moment you start writing songs, whether you are interested in film and TV placement or not, become a member of a performance rights organization as a songwriter and a publisher and register your songs. If you're not a member of a PRO, and your songs are not registered with the PRO, you will not receive any performance royalties.

Many independent artists have already at completed (part of) this first step, reaching out to ASCAP, BMI or SESAC and becoming a songwriter member of one of these organizations. However, we frequently encounter writers who fail to become **publisher** members too. At BMI, if you're not a publisher member, and your songs get performed, BMI will pay you 200%, i.e. 100% of both the publisher and songwriter's share of performance income. At both SESAC and ASCAP, you must also be a publisher member or you'll miss out on the publisher share of performance income.

Becoming a publisher member of a PRO requires a separate membership (and fee) from the songwriter membership. You don't have to be an official "business," LLC or S Corp to set up your **publishing entity.** You can do so using your social security number and making up a publisher name when joining.

Publishing Entity - A publishing entity can be attached to an established publishing company or merely a fictitious company name set up by a songwriter who owns his or her own publishing. Performance rights societies pay songwriter royalties to songwriters and publishing royalties to publishing entities.

The PRO you choose to join will be able to advise further on this process, and both ASCAP and BMI have very helpful FAQ pages with regards to membership.

Performance rights organizations have much more to offer than just royalty collection and distribution and title registration. They're communities of like-minded songwriters and musicians that offer networking and collaboration opportunities throughout the country. They host panels, showcases and industry conferences in various cities where you can learn and meet people, including music supervisors and other gatekeepers to getting music placed in media. Once you've joined, contact your representative and spending time learning more and getting involved.

How does this affect the job of a music supervisor? PRO websites (ASCAP and BMI) are frequently the first stop when researching publishing rights for a song. Our jobs are significantly easier if the information, both company names and contact details, are accurate and up to date. While registration is not technically required for song clearance, not registering makes it harder for a music supervisor to track down publishing contact information, therefore making it harder to clear the song. It does not matter which organization you are registered with, or if your co-writers are with different organizations, as long as the song is registered.

Other resources used to research publishing ownership include Harry Fox, US Copyright Office, Wikipedia, other performing rights organizations around the world, and regular old Google.

If all goes well, contact information can be found on either the various websites listed above or a band, label or other website. But if not, then the search continues...sometimes even going as far as to call names in the yellow pages. Remember what we said about 100% of both sides needing to be cleared in order to use a song? Even if the company or person who controls only 1% of the publishing on a song cannot be found, we will have to move on from the song.

And then comes the paperwork...

Quote Request Letters

Once a music supervisor has tracked down all the parties that control the master recording and publishing rights to a song (also called the "Licensors"), each party is sent a **quote request letter,** with as much information as possible about the use of the song and the song itself (e.g. writers, artist, publishing company). The following information is standard for both master recording and publishing quote request letters. While technically both are "synchronization" requests over time the word "synchronization" has become primarily associated with the publishing side and has stuck. Therefore, you will likely receive either a master use or synchronization quote request letter depending on what you represent (and a combined quote request letter if you control both the master recording and the publishing).

It's important to note again that this is not the final license paperwork - quote request letters include only the essential information and as such are often very simple. It is only after the use is happening (i.e. "confirmed") and the license is drafted that additional language is added and finer points discussed and negotiated.

BOTH MASTER AND SYNCHRONIZATION QUOTE REQUEST LETTERS WILL INCLUDE:

1. Song Title

2. Type of Use - Song uses in media typically fall into four broad categories:

- Background Vocal - A vocal section of a recorded song is being used to picture. This can be either diegetic (music on a car radio, waiting room, elevator, etc.) or non-diegetic (montage or transition).
- Background Instrumental - Same as above, except instrumental only. If a vocal audio track is being used but the section heard in the picture is instrumental only (an introduction, for example) the use is still instrumental.
- Visual Vocal - A song with vocals is performed on

camera. This includes a rock concert/band, choir, someone humming a tune, singing along to the radio, etc.

- Visual Instrumental - An instrumental song is performed on camera, like an orchestra or a string quartet.

Some music supervisors will use "featured" or "montage" in describing the use, but more often than not, those words will appear in the "Scene Description" area. If a song is heard during the "Main Titles" (played over the opening credits) or "End Titles" (played over the end credit roll) that information will also be specified here (e.g. Main Titles / Background Vocal).

3. Scene Description - What is being seen on screen while the song is heard? Is it a montage? Is it playing on a car radio in the background during a conversation? Occasionally filmmakers will assume that "clearing" a song gives them the right to use it wherever, for however long and however many times they want in a film, when really it is only cleared for the specific scene requested. If a song is used twice, both uses need to be cleared, and the descriptions for both scenes included - with the occasional exception of the "interrupted use".

If a song is used more than once in what is essentially the same scene or with only a brief pause, it may be considered "interrupted". For example, a girl is on the phone at a concert and the scenes cut back and forth from the venue (where music is playing) and her mom on the other end at home (no music playing). The song in the venue would likely be cleared as one interrupted use, with a timing that is the aggregate of all the parts where the song can be heard at the venue. Alternately, if three or four scenes later the girl goes back to the venue and the same song can be heard again, that is a new scene and a new use.

4. Timing - How long a song can be heard in the picture. This will affect the price of the song, as there is a big difference between using 2 seconds and 2 minutes. While price increases tend to occur when timings cross the full minute thresholds e.g. the 1-minute, 2-minute, 3-minute marks, there are no strict increments, and it depends on the overall music budget. This means that sometimes a higher timing can mean a few hundred dollars more for a lower budget project, or a couple thousand more if the budget is higher.

5. Term - The desired length of time for the song to be licensed. Often this is "in perpetuity" but depending on the media, a more limited term may be more appropriate, e.g. one year (often the case for film festival rights), two years, five years, ten years.

6. Territory - The desired territory in which a song is to be cleared. For example, if a television series will only be shown within the United States, then the song only needs to be cleared for use within the United States. If the series or content will be distributed worldwide, then the Territory would be worldwide. It does happen that ownership rights can be divided up by territory. For example,

Company A may control 100% of the song in the United States and Canada, and Company B may control 100% of the song in the Rest of the World (i.e. World excluding the United States and Canada). If your project will air or be seen throughout the entire world, both Company A and Company B will need to approve the use (again, the magic number is 100%). Territory splits can easily get more complicated, but again, these are the basics.

7. Media Rights Requested - Detailing out the array of possible rights situations could be an entire chapter. In it's simplest form this can be described as where the project (within which the song will be contained i.e. synchronized) will be seen/distributed. Is it a television show that will be on various forms of television (network, cable, premium cable) and streamed online? Is it a film that will be in theaters where patrons buy tickets to see the film? Will it be only on streaming platforms like Netflix, or can consumers download the product and keep it for themselves? The current standard language for most films will be, "All media now known or hereafter devised," and for television, "All media now known or hereafter devised excluding theatrical," though with the changing media landscape and distribution methods, that is starting to break down further (e.g. Internet Streaming Only, Video On Demand services, Download-To-Own or Electronic Sell Through, etc.)

It's also common to see mentions of advertising and promo rights in connection with the film in this section. "In-context promos" would be the use of the exact scene that containing the song in a promotional way; the song will be used in exactly the same way as it is in the context of the film. "Out-of-context" promos are much less often included in standard quote requests – these pertain to the use of the song in a different context than it is used in the film, such as trailers. While "in-context" rights are frequently rolled into a standard quote request for an in-film or in-show use, "out-of-context" rights require an additional fee.

Most of the time in film and television these rights are non-exclusive, meaning that you can grant synchronization rights to use a song in multiple projects at the same time, such as a film and a television show. Given the branding component of trailers and advertisements however, you may see language requesting "exclusive" rights, meaning that if the song is used in an IKEA advertisement it cannot be used in any other media (or at least similar media, like another advertisement or for a similar product which is called "product exclusivity') for a certain period of time. Exclusivity is also sometimes requested for important songs in major films, such as something created original for the project or an end titles use.

While every element above is taken into consideration, territory, term and the requested media rights are the three key elements in determining the cost of the song.

SYNCHRONIZATION QUOTE REQUEST LETTERS WILL ALSO INCLUDE:

- Songwriter Names
- Publishing Entity Names (Typically found on the PRO or Harry Fox websites)

MASTER QUOTE REQUEST LETTERS WILL ALSO INCLUDE:

- Artist Name
- Album Title (Sometimes, but not always)
- Record Label Name (Sometimes, but not always)

If there is any language you feel is essential to your feeling comfortable with the use, by all means write it on the quote request letter – most still do this by hand! Or conversely, if there is language on the request you are not comfortable agreeing to, it is your prerogative to cross something out. Be aware, however, that if the requested use is for a project with a major studio behind it (e.g. Fox, Sony, ABC, NBC, Universal) it's possible that crossing out certain language could be a deal-breaker.

The moment a quote request is sent out a clock starts ticking and the anxiety begins. Television, in particular, calls for especially quick turnarounds, as sometimes I won't get a script until a day or two before the episode starts shooting. Post Production on an episode might only last a week. That's a very limited time to make collaborative creative choices, pursue song clearances and troubleshoot if any issues arise. Add to that how sometimes directors or producers might make last minute changes within hours of finishing an episode or the eleventh hour on a film, and it's easy to see why "fast and easy clearance" is a selling point for emerging companies and artists pitching music for film and television.

This is not always the case, but it can be. Film tends to allow for more breathing room in the clearance process, however no one likes to be kept in limbo very long. Regardless of the timeline, or whether the answer is "yes" or "no," respond as quickly as possible to either ease everyone's minds...or establish it's time to move on to the next before anyone gets too attached.

But what about the money?

Depending on the situation, a music supervisor may write in a suggested or preferred fee, or leave a blank line for the licensor to write in their quote (i.e. your desired fee for the use). Keep in mind that even if it is not specified, it is assumed that this fee will be **based on 100% of the ownership of that "side" of the cue.** Whether it's specified on the paperwork or not, publishers quote based on 100% of the publishing rights, and master owners quote based on 100% of the master recording. Exceptions do sometimes arise with samples or side artist approval, but that is for another book.

For example, if the suggested fee for the publishing is
$5,000.00 (i.e. what is written by the music supervisor or
clearance person on the quote request) and you control
50% of the publishing, you would be owed $2,500.00. If
you were to write in "$5,000.00" and controlled 50% of
the publishing it would be assumed (unless specifically
indicated) that you agree to receiving $2,500.00 for your
share.

It may seem crazy to those who control 100% of the master
recordings and publishing on their songs, but it regularly
happens that the master recording owner and publisher (or
co-publishers) are different companies and *do not communicate* on quote requests that come in. Often ownership
parties quote different fees. The master recording owner
may quote $10,000.00 for use of the master recording, one
co-publisher $7,500.00 based on 100% of the publishing,
and another $15,000.00 for the same use.

Then what happens? To ensure all parties are paid fairly
based on their shares, licensors will typically add language
to their approvals citing that the fee quoted is on a "most
favored nations" (a/k/a MFN) basis with the master
recording owner and/or co-publishers. Let's say one of the
publishers quotes $7,500.00, and another publisher quotes
$15,000.00. If the lower-quoting licensor writes "most
favored nations with the master and co-publishers" on their
approval, it essentially makes it the same as if the lower
quoting licensor had also quoted $15,000.00. Using the
numbers from the example, if they controlled 50% of the
publishing they would now be owed $7,500.00, instead of

$3,750.00. This is when a music supervisor might call the licensor who quoted the highest amount and try to negotiate a lower fee. The bottom line when it comes to MFN: if one licensor quotes higher and gets paid more than the rest, the fees go up across the board.

As with everything in the music clearance process, there are exceptions. In certain situations, a music supervisor might ask a licensor to "remove the MFN", often to keep the project on budget. Covers, for example, are sometimes cleared on a "non-MFN basis" when it is a cover of a well-known song created by an unknown band. An iconic songwriter may quote $25,000 for the publishing on their hit song, but Joe Smith will agree to $2,000 for the use of his recording of that song.

It should also be noted that the numbers above are not "standard" by any means. Fees are extremely dependent on the type of media (television, film, trailers, etc.) and budget of the project. More on that to come later in this book.

CONFIRMATION LETTERS AND LICENSE REQUESTS

Again, no use is locked until you are explicitly told that the project is completed and the song was used. Once all songs are cleared, final selections have been made, and a film or television show has finished it's "final mix and playback" or "printmastered" (i.e. is completely done, there will be no more changes)...then the confirmation and licensing process can begin. In an ideal world, a music supervisor would notify the artist or pitching company as soon as they know a song is (or isn't) being used, but unfortunately other urgent deadlines and needs frequently get in the way. The date most of us keep an eye toward is the air or premiere date.

The information agreed upon in the quote request letter - term, territory, media rights, fee - forms the foundation of the **license**. Licenses also include additional language regarding warranties and representations, indemnification, assignments, and (for film and television) obligations regarding cue sheets, end credits, and performance rights society payments. The terms will, of course, vary based on the media (commercials, promos, film, television, video games, etc.) A benefit of working with a label, publisher or third-party pitching company is that they will likely have their own preferred license form and legal team to use on your behalf.

When dealing with a company, especially a major label or publisher (rather than an independent artist), music supervisors often send out a **confirmation letter** (also sometimes called a **"license request"**) rather than a long form license. This letter confirms the terms already agreed upon in the quote request letter as well as any details that may have fluctuated between initial clearance and final mix, such as the timing and the fee. Maybe the song was cleared for two minutes, but only one minute and 23 seconds were used.

If it happens that the final fee is higher than what you quoted or agreed to on the request, it likely means that another ownership party (master, co-publisher, etc.) quoted higher than you, and the "most favored nations" provision kicked in. You are therefore owed an equivalent amount (i.e. a higher fee), based on 100% of the quote.

The confirmation letter can be as formal as a mini-agreement, or as informal as an email confirming the song was (or will be) indeed used and the agreed upon terms and fee(s). Sometimes major studios will craft their confirmation letter template to serve as the license itself. Often though, the licensor will respond by sending their preferred license agreement to the studio or production company for signature. If you are an independent artist without such a template on hand, feel free to request the production company send their preferred paperwork for your review.

Once confirmation letters are sent, it is common for the production company, producer and production lawyer or studio to take over the process from the music supervisor.

Different companies and studios each handle licensing and payment their own way. Typically, they will be clear as to the next steps, such as whether the licensor should issue a license and/or invoice for payment. Some will await a signed license from the licensor before issuing payment. Since these are legal contracts, it does happen that negotiating the finer points of a license can take time. Lawyers sometimes go back and forth for years without agreeing upon language for situations that may or may not occur down the line.

Fortunately, this will not necessarily hold up payment. There are a few important details however, to keep in mind about the payment process.

1. As noted above, the licensing and payment process is triggered when it is confirmed that a song will be used. In film, this is generally after the final mix, which often happens months (sometimes years) after a song is initially cleared. In television, confirmation letters are typically sent around the episode airdate. There are exceptions of course, but the scenarios above are most common.

2. Payment can only be issued when the percentages add up to exactly 100%. As we've discussed at length, a song is not considered cleared until 100% of the master recording and publishing rights-holders have approved. If less than 100% approve, then you are likely missing a party. Sometimes though, the percentages wind up equaling more than 100%. In these situations, the song is usually considered cleared and can be used...however, even if the splits are just 0.1% over 100%, a studio cannot issue payment to anyone and will request the licensors work out an adjustment.

3. Large companies or studios are handling

accounting for multiple films and television shows. Checks aren't turned around in a day. The typical process time is 90 – 120 days after the episode airs, though sometimes it can be sooner.

4. Similarly, large companies - and many smaller ones - require tax forms, vendor forms and invoices. If the licensor or business name on the contract, invoice and required forms don't all match, it could delay payment.

THE MUSIC CUE SHEET

The final task of a music supervisor is ensuring the music cue sheet is completed accurately. A **music cue sheet** is a list of all songs and score cues in a project a chronological list of all songs and score cues in a project as heard in the picture. Essential information includes the release date of the project, song titles, composer names, publisher names, songwriter and publishing ownership percentages, timings and the type of use (as described above). The final music cue sheet is distributed to the performance rights societies. ASCAP then matches the song titles with those registered by ASCAP writers and publishers in their database. BMI and SESAC do the same. Each organization then tracks when projects air and when songs are used and distributes performance royalties to songwriters and publishers for the public performance of their works. Foreign performance rights societies (PRS in England, SACEM in France, GEMA in Germany, etc.) do the same and work in tandem with ASCAP, BMI and SESAC and publishing companies to track overseas revenue as well.

Typically, whoever is responsible for song clearance (music supervisor, studio clearance department, clearance professional) is in turn responsible for assembling relevant cue sheet information. If a music supervisor is not responsible for clearance, they will likely still check everything over to make sure the songs are in the correct order and no last minute changes occurred that aren't reflected on the cue sheet. Often the information is then passed along to a music editor who will have the most accurate list of cues and timings and add the songwriter and publisher information into their preferred cue sheet template or program. In the absence of a music editor, however, assembling the information will fall onto the music supervisor. Again, it is essential all songs are registered correctly with the relevant performing rights societies, and that accurate information is provided to the music supervisor so that songwriters and music publishers will get paid their performance royalties.

In summation, music supervisors rely upon (and are relied upon for) speed, thoroughness and accuracy in this facet of the job. The artists, songwriters and companies I work with regularly are those who deliver consistently so I can, in turn, deliver for clients.

2 ASSEMBLING YOUR TOOLBOX

Now you have some awareness of the expected from a Music Supervisor and what is needed from an artist/writer or company pitching music, how do you begin to meet those needs? Increasing the odds of your music being used in film and television has just as much to do with preparation as the song itself. Even the best, most creatively "perfect" song can lose a placement if the artist or pitching company is not armed with the necessary knowledge and a myriad of ancillary elements.

Since you have already joined your PRO of choice as a writer and publisher, and you have a basic understanding of the two "sides" of a song as well as the clearance process, this chapter will provide a step by step overview of the creative and technical elements every artist interested in having their music placed in media should consider **before, during and after** recording a song, including production quality, stems, metadata tagging and more. If you represent a catalog, it may be helpful to pass this along to your greener clients; after all it's in your best interest to ensure each song and artist is properly prepared to pitch and to help facilitate wherever you can.

BEFORE YOU GET INTO THE STUDIO

What makes a song "sync-able?" Music supervisors are regularly asked how we like to receive music submissions, how to stand out in emails, what our preferred delivery services are and so on - however, a song that's great for sync begins in the songwriting process. Not every song is right for sync – some of my favorite songs of all time fall into that category – and that is completely fine! First and foremost, you should be making the music that you are inspired to make and that creatively fulfills you. However, If you are interested in having your music placed in media - and it's assumed you are if you've sought out this book- then there are certain parameters to be aware of that will help get you closer to your goal.

For one, different media have different needs. Advertisements, for example, regularly seek music with good energy and positive lyrics. Trailers use many more instrumental only cues than film and television, and the music often actually drives the "story" (or edit) – whereas, in film and television it's the opposite. When considering whether or not a song will work in film or television, it is important to keep in mind that the goal of the filmmaker, and in turn the music supervisor, is to use music to tell their story. The song ultimately needs to support the characters and story being told on screen. Will your song enhance the moment or distract?

While there are a variety of classes, seminars and conferences specifically geared to the techniques of creating songs for media, here are some brief insights from top music supervisors on what they are listening for:

1. Varied instrumental arrangement. Rapping or singing over a loop or repetitive beat can get tiresome played over a long scene. Make sure there are several "builds" and/or changes throughout your song (without giving it split personality disorder) that might help support a sequence with several changes in pacing or tone.

2. Room to breathe (and therefore edit). It's rare that a song fits perfectly into a scene as is. Almost always some editing is needed to finesse the two together – perhaps that's starting on a certain note for a more impactful introduction, ensuring a certain lyric lands on the right action, dropping out a vocal line or two to make sure a dialogue is heard, etc. If your lyrics are rapid fire with extremely few instrumental moments, it can make it very difficult for the music supervisor or Music Editor to create the perfect marriage, so err on the sparse side.

3. A consistent message. It is easier to find homes for songs where the lyrical content and tone are in harmony (e.g. an upbeat song that has positive lyrics) as opposed to when there is incongruence between the two (e.g. calm sounding song with angry lyrics, or a happy ukulele song with depressing lyrics). This is not to say such a song can't be a subversive choice for the right moment, those opportunities just come up less frequently. A well-defined, straightforward hook is much more versatile than an abstract approach.

4. A distinct and attention-grabbing feel. In advertising, songs need to make an impact in thirty seconds or less, so long slow builds are difficult to work with, particularly in this medium.

5. High quality or "broadcast ready" production. I will get into this shortly, but demos are no longer acceptable unless you are asked specifically for a demo. Even then most demos these days are turned in incredibly fleshed out.

6. A unique take on universal themes (love, heartbreak, home, togetherness, strength, forgiveness, etc.) If you think about it, the crux of most films, television shows and advertisements can be distilled into one of these universal emotions, so it stands to reason that songs with one at the core will have ample opportunities for placement. Of course, while "love" might be universal, you are your own artist and person with your own personal experience and perspective, and that's what we're looking for. Music supervisors always appreciate songs about love that are not romantic such as the love between siblings, family, friends, or of life in general.

Conversely, songs with lyrics that are too specific and descriptive (e.g. *"I woke up and looked out my window / Snow covers the ground / I pour my coffee and read the paper..."*) are extremely hard to place. The visual nature of lyrics like these will likely distract from what the viewer is seeing on screen. Along these lines, proper nouns - cities or other places, or names of people - in lyrics also present a challenge.

7. Authenticity and sincerity. At the end of the day, it's clear when a song, performance or mix is phoned in - when it's obvious those involved were just going through the motions of what they thought would be successful. Having a genuine, distinct, confident voice and perspective is the necessary foundation to build upon; those who do that rise to the top of the pile no matter where (or to whom) you are sending your music.

This is just the tip of the iceberg, but when it comes down to it, a great song will always stand out even if it does not tick every box listed above. For feedback on whether your work is hitting these marks, I recommend attending conferences such as the following:

- MUSEXPO (Los Angeles, CA)
- Guild Of Music Supervisors State of Music in Media Conference (Los Angeles, CA)
- ASCAP I Create Music EXPO (Los Angeles, CA)
- Durango Songwriters Expo (Ventura & Santa Ynez, CA and Durango, CO)

- South by Southwest (SXSW) Music Conference
  (Austin, TX)

And of course, any event held by organizations you are involved in that is focused on providing feedback on songs, including many hosted by the Association of Independent Music Publishers (AIMP), National Association of Record Industry Professionals (NARIP) or the Society of Composers & Lyricists (SCL), which happen all over the country.

Can't afford to attend? Pay close attention to the songs you love that have found their way into film, television, advertisements or trailers or even radio – what are they about and what is their structure? Why is it working? Listen for patterns in the lyrics and instrumentation.

Covers

Something else to consider when deciding what to record: covers. Music supervisors frequently turn to covers for either a fresh take on a known tune or because an original master recording is too expensive (or both), so it never hurts to have a couple awesome covers in your back pocket. When approaching a cover however, strive to put your own mark on the song rather than replicating the original. It doesn't need to be a drastic change; it just needs to feel authentically you.

Choose your covers wisely as certain writers or artists won't allow covers to be used, or the publishing is so complicated or cost prohibitive, any potential use of the cover would be automatically killed. If you are signed to a pitching company or label, they can help provide guidance on what covers are worth pursuing. That said, it's not a bad idea to try and reach out to the "sync" team (those responsible for pitching songs for various media) at a major publisher for their suggestions of songs to cover. They will be able to advise on what songs are regularly requested, are easily cleared on the publishing side, and/or have an expensive or difficult original master recording owner. Want another approach if you are on your own? Research whether or not the song you are interested in covering has been used in film or television before. This book will dive further into research sources shortly, but if a song is frequently used in media, it's likely that it is easy to clear.

WHILE YOU ARE IN THE STUDIO

1. Make it sound good. This may seem obvious, but it is not. To compete with label quality music, your music needs to be label quality.

I'm not here to provide technical recording tips or recommend studios or Producers to call, but it is worth the effort and money to find a good studio or producer to work with. Maybe that producer is you. Maybe your garage has been converted to a killer recording studio. Whatever the case may be, with such an abundance of technology and equipment available to the general public, not only is there a glut of music out there, much of it actually sounds decent. This makes sparse or shoddy production or strictly computerized beats and samples stand out immediately - and not in a good way. These days, there is no excuse for cheap sounding music so invest in whatever will result in the highest quality.

Having said that, "label" or "broadcast" quality can mean different things depending on the genre. Katy Perry is different from M83 is different from The Orwells is different from The Joy Formidable is different from Kurt Vile. Listen to music by the artists at the level you aspire to reach on the radio stations or platforms you want your music played (be it KROQ or KCRW). Then listen to your music. Strive to make the production quality sound the same as your idols (or competitors).

2. Create clean versions. This is only applicable to artists who use inappropriate language in their songs and more of a suggestion than an instruction at that. If explicit lyrics are part of your brand, and bleeping songs would turn them into Morse code messages, then it may not make sense to create a clean version unless it's with different lyrics entirely. If that's the case, however, don't expect your music to be used in network television shows or family films. There are "standards and practices" rules against the use of certain words. If you are edgy, but have a huge teen audience (Nicki Minaj for example), it's wise to have clean versions available. Basically, the less swear words used in a song - or the easier it is for an editor to "cut around" the swear words (i.e. use only the clean sections of a song, avoiding those lyrics with explicit language) - the more doors are open for that song to be used in film and television, particularly on network and basic cable.

3. Create sample free versions. Again, this is only applicable if you are the type of artist interested in using samples. Are you using a sample of a master recording by the original artist, or re-recording a lyric or guitar lick? Yes, quoting a lyric in your song is considered sample use. Both types of samples require different deals in place before a song can be licensed. With that in mind, and especially if you are an emerging artist, try to stay away from sample use entirely or at least avoid samples from major artists or of popular songs. You should also make sure to create a version without the sample. If you plan to use a sample from an Etta James song in yours, for example, it will be significantly easier to clear if you record another female vocal singing her lyric rather than using an Etta James recording owned by a major label. You will only have to "clear" (get permission to use or in this case, incorporate) the composition. An arrangement will still need to be made with the publisher for the use of the copyright, but the less hurdles the better. Be aware though that in clearing the publishing for a sample use, it's likely (and common) that the publisher of the sample will own and control a percentage of the new composition. So, even if you create a sample free version of that song, they are still co-owners and any use (synch or otherwise) will still need to be cleared with them as well.

AFTER YOU'VE LEFT THE STUDIO

Having the stellar-sounding, completed full track is obviously important, but not enough. As mentioned earlier, it's rare a song fits to picture as is; some editing is usually needed to finesse the union, beyond just cutting out explicit words.

Often these edits include making tracks shorter by taking out a verse or chorus, using only a few lines, using only the beginning or end, and so forth. The right to make such edits is included in most standard song clearance paperwork. What is *not* typically included is any edit that constitutes changing the fundamental nature of a song, for example "non-linear editing" (moving the first verse to the end, continuously looping verses, etc.), changing the lyrics, cutting out every other line and so forth. Sometimes production companies will seek to include these rights, however, be aware that it is the exception and not the rule.

In order to give your music the best chance at landing a placement, it benefits you to have certain materials on hand that are key to facilitating the first, "good" type of editing. Every artist or company pitching music should have all of the following ancillary items readily available. Often I reach out requesting one or more of these items and am told that it needs to be procured from a studio, producer or other source. If it takes more than a couple hours to send an instrumental only version of a track you could lose the placement. So, ensure you are in possession of all of the items below before leaving (or shortly after you leave) the studio:

1. Gather multiple file types of different versions. This includes...

- **Stems.** Most importantly, make sure you have instrumental only and "a cappella" (vocals only) versions of every song. These are often necessary for Editors to make a song fit smoothly against picture or in transitions. More stems are always appreciated; without percussion or without melody are both good ones to have as well. If more elaborate stems are requested, however, it is within your rights to get more information on how those will be used. Most music supervisors respect the integrity of the music and will police stem use for you, but if the request is coming from someone without a proven track record, you should inquire further.
- **MP3 and AIF files.** While M4A or WAV files will also be accepted, some Editors have said that MP3 and AIF files work better with AVID. MP3 files can be created fairly easily in iTunes using the "MP3 Encoder", but lower quality files cannot be converted to higher quality (e.g. from MP3 to WAV or AIF, which are uncompressed, high-quality file types). Always make sure you have high-quality versions ready and able to be sent quickly. Hi-resolution versions of all stems

(instrumental only, a cappella, etc.) are important
to have as well.

- **TV Mix.** A TV Mix is a version of the song
  often created by request, and respectively can
  mean different things to different people.
  Sometimes a "TV mix" is the same as the clean
  version. Sometimes it is a shorter version of the
  song that gets into the chorus much faster, or cuts
  out any meandering solos. Many consider it a
  version that is mostly instrumental, with the only
  lyrics being the chorus, as well as claps, stomps,
  "ooh's" or "ah's" (depending on the song, of
  course). Because of the differing needs and
  opinions, it's not typically expected that an artist
  have one at the ready. However if you feel your
  music could benefit from having an alternate mix,
  it may be worth looking into. At the end of the
  day, the more versions of a song you have in your
  back pocket the quicker and more likely you will
  be to meet any need thrown your way.

**2. Type up your lyrics, and then make them
easily accessible.** If a music supervisor cannot understand the lyrics to your song and can't find them anywhere,
it is possible that song will be promptly deleted. Or kept
and continually passed over for every music search, unsure
if the lyrics actually fit what is happening on screen (or are
even appropriate). Studios also often require lyrics to be
submitted for standards and practices.

Do yourself a favor and ensure that the official lyrics are somewhere easily accessible, preferably on your own website so a music supervisor can find them even if we are working on an urgent music search at 10pm on a Saturday (this happens). If for some reason that's not an option, or you're not comfortable with posting them publicly, make sure you and/or anyone who is pitching your music has PDFs at the ready. Some companies and artists even embed lyrics in the metadata of the audio file (more on metadata shortly) which is always appreciated.

3. Sort out writer and publishing ownership.
The discussion of writer splits as mentioned in the last chapter could (and often does) happen after a song or even album is completed, but it may be prudent to have it much earlier - before getting too deep into the work - so there are no cases of mistaken expectations. That said, we are fully aware changes can happen during the creative process between writing and receiving a final mastered track. One song can go through many evolutions.

For one reason or another it does happen that writer splits take months to work out (especially with major label artists and the in rap/hip hop genres in particular). Remember that the faster these are confirmed the easier the job is for the music supervisor and the faster you will get paid. Again, most studios will not issue any payment until splits add up to 100% exactly. And a happy music supervisor will yield more opportunities for you.

4. Register your song on with your PRO (ASCAP, BMI or SESAC). As detailed in the last chapter, it is essential to be a member of a performance rights organization as a writer *and* a publisher, otherwise you may be leaving royalty money on the table. It is recommended that a song be registered as soon as writer and publisher splits are confirmed.

5. Add metadata to the audio files. This step is required whether you are an artist, own an indie pitching company or man the catalog of a major label or publishing company, and will come up more than once before this book is complete. Metadata is an essential tool music supervisors use and rely upon to catalog, track and search their personal music libraries. Not having the correct metadata can result in your song getting passed over for a music search and consequently you'll lose out on potential income. As it's been said several times, if a song can't be cleared, it can't be used - and if a music supervisor cannot identify the rights holders, they cannot clear the song. While music supervisors utilize metadata in a variety of ways, clearance contact information is perhaps the most vital.

The Importance of Metadata

Alright, so what is metadata? It's all the information embedded in a track: song title, artist name, album name, BPM, etc. On the most rudimentary level, if you go into your iTunes and right click (or Control click) on a track and select "Song Info" you will see various *metadata* fields pop up with such information.

Those who are hired to embed such data professionally use more layered and comprehensive programs like Sound-miner, but the majority of music supervisors aren't using anything more sophisticated than iTunes (or Swinsian, which looks very similar to iTunes in design).

While no two music supervisors are exactly alike in how they organize data in their own libraries, there are some easy to follow guidelines that will put you ahead of many peers:

1. Don't forget the basics, such as track names, artist names and album names (more on these below). Believe it or not general music email blasts and search submissions from major labels and publishers are sometimes missing artist names.

2. Contact information, including your name, company, phone number and email address is essential – your mailing address is not. Typically, this is embedded at the start of the Comments section or the Grouping field for company name. Different music supervisors have different preferences here, however, Company Name in either Grouping or Comments is very common.

3. Ownership information, including names of master recording owner and publishing company, is extremely help-ful. To the same point as above, to clear a song, a music supervisor needs to know both who to go to and how to reach them. Ownership details inform the former, so we appreciate any and all information you're able to provide.

At the very least, it's extremely helpful for us to know whether or not you are representing the master recording, the publishing or both. If you are a singer-songwriter who wrote all of your own songs and recorded them yourself in your home studio, then you likely own 100% of the master recording and publishing. Songs where 100% of the master recording and publishing rights are controlled by one person or company are often called "one stop", meaning you only need to go to one person to clear and license the song. To use in context:

"The Way I Am" by Ingrid Michaelson can be cleared one stop through Secret Road Music Services"

If you want to go as far as indicating what *percentage* of the master recording or publishing rights you control as well, that's even better. It's not uncommon for pitching companies to include their "side" and ownership percentage in the iTunes Comments field (e.g. "Hidden Track Music (Master Only)" or "Ocean Park Music Group = 50% Publishing"). If you want bonus points though, also include the percentages and company names of the *other rights-holders* in the song. Music supervisors will be impressed and appreciative, and this will increase your chances of getting a placement. After all, if a song needs to be cleared urgently, and the music supervisor cannot figure out the name of the third writer or publisher - that's money you will be losing out on even if your contact information is easily accessible. If you can easily provide that information, you've saved the day for all parties.

That said, in certain deal structures (which we will go into later in this book), getting your commission is predicated on being the person or company who pitches the song for a particular project. If you find yourself in such a situation, seek to asterisk, capitalize or otherwise uniquely highlight your information, or put the other rights-holders after yours in parentheses, so the metadata is clear about where the file came from. If not, then at least having this information (and contact details) on hand when we ask would be hugely helpful.

4. Don't forget about album name, and don't change the album to be the name of a sampler. This is especially important for songs that appear (or will appear) on multiple albums. Sometimes artists will self-release an album, and then get signed to a record label and re-record or re-master certain tracks. Music supervisors also frequently get sent the same song from multiple companies, and album name (along with song duration) helps identify whether we are receiving a new version or the exact same track from different sources.

At the end of the day, the music supervisor needs to know exactly which master is being sent to the editor so we know which version to clear.

5. Fill out as many fields as available. Composer (i.e. Songwriter), Year (i.e. the year the recording was released), BPM and Genre are all details that may not be essential for clearance, but many music supervisors find these details extremely useful. I have had to tap out BPM or take release date into account for many a song search. If you have them on hand, include not only the songwriter names in the Composer field but their PRO affiliation and songwriter percentages as well. Again, these aren't essential for clearance, but can prove extremely valuable in certain situations.

6. Use strategic keywords where you can. In iTunes, the Genre and Comments sections are both frequently used to hold keywords. Yes, this is incredibly subjective, but including even just one or two keywords addressing the theme ("cheating," "starting over"), genre ("Pop Rock") and/or mood ("bitter," "cathartic") will be a much-appreciated head start in categorizing the song. Try not to overdo it though; an entire thesaurus of synonyms for "happy" is unnecessary.

One descriptor that is extremely helpful: similar artists (e.g. Sounds like Rihanna). Searching "pop" in an iTunes library can yield hundreds of results, many not even close to the creative need like songs or albums with the word in the title. Artist names, however, are usually specific enough to only invoke songs by or featuring the artist, and anything specifically tagged as similar.

Whatever descriptive keywords you choose to describe and embed in your music, please be honest. It is a constant frustration when tracks are misrepresented by an artist or pitching company. If necessary, solicit a fellow musician who may help provide some perspective, and limit yourself to only the 5 - 6 most apt descriptors.

7. Pay attention to grammar and formatting. If you are unsure how your metadata will appear, drop the file into an iTunes library and see what comes up. Most music supervisors want information presented in as clear and concise a way as possible with minimal work on their part. If the way you've added your data results in a huge gap in the Comments section, for example, you should probably tweak it. Please make sure nothing IS IN ALL CAPS, and please do not lump all the information into one field (e.g. song title, artist name, company name and email all in the Name field).

8. Include any other important notes a music supervisor may need to know about a track, and make sure to mention if it is watermarked or unreleased. Many artists and pitching companies will include such disclaimers in the body of the email when sending music. This is still recommended, but the huge volume of music (and emails) downloaded and processed every day makes it easy to lose track of these details. If "UNRELEASED" or "WATERMARKED" appears very clearly in the Comments or Album section when importing into iTunes, you can be sure the information won't be forgotten when working on a search three months later. Similarly, it is also good to know upfront when tracks are demos or unfinished or if instrumentals or a clean version (if applicable) are not available.

One last note on metadata... MP3 and AIF files will carry metadata, but WAV versions will not. Even if you add the metadata in iTunes and drag the file into a folder on your Desktop, the file will not retain the information.

Once you have a catalog of music you are proud of and excited about and are prepped and ready for any request thrown at you - from stems to lyrics - you are ready to move on to the next step: approaching those with the power to get your music in media!

3 PLANNING YOUR APPROACH: RESEARCH, TECHNOLOGY & ETIQUETTE

They say that in entertainment (and really in any industry) it's not what you know, it's who you know. Whoever "they" are, they are absolutely correct. What makes gaining a foothold in the entertainment industry especially tricky is the heavy emphasis on the social aspect. In the music world, many of our most important interactions take place at concerts, in music venues, or at artist showcases, with a drink in hand.

Now that you have assembled your toolbox, this chapter will introduce some of the different players you will encounter in the film and television music world and the most effective ways to approach them.

In large part due to the ocean of music coming to music supervisors daily, knowing *how* to pitch your music is an important component in getting it placed. When I say ocean it is not hyperbole – dozens of music submissions from artists, managers, labels, publishers, etc. come in every single day. While I don't know anyone who will use bad music just because they like the person who sent it to them, many music supervisors will screen calls and delete emails from pitch people and artists who don't "get it." Standing out is good, but appearing obnoxious, pushy, entitled or just plain rude is not.

If you are an artist already working with a label, publisher or third-party pitching company, you're a step ahead of the game. You have at least one person on your team who (presumably) has the right knowledge, experience and relationships to get your music into the right hands, reaching out to and courting music supervisors and executives on your behalf.

Still, it is always wise for an artist to be prepared in the event you run into a potential business contact at a house party, out at a show or even at a friend's dinner party. You never know when a personal connection will lead to an opportunity, and it is always a good idea to be proactive when it comes to your own career - if you proceed with discretion.

Because of how often music industry folks conduct business in social settings, "business relationships" are far more personal than in other fields, though equally essential. For a music supervisor, the right relationships with a label or publisher could mean lower fees and faster turnaround on a clearance. One pitching company might be sent a music search that another company doesn't receive. An artist may be given an opportunity to write an end title song for a film because of a mutual friend. Relationships are currency. The more people you not only get to know, but get to trust and like you both for your music *and* your personality, the better off you will be.

This is the most vital and difficult piece of the puzzle to navigate piece of the puzzle for someone pitching music. Far more complicated than adjusting to supervisors' varying delivery requirements (though those will be addressed as well) is figuring out how to interact with each of them as human beings. How do you create and nurture this unique type of "business friendship?"

There is no "right" way of course. You don't become best friends with every person you meet after all. Everyone connects with people differently, on different levels, for different reasons, and understanding that is key as you wade into this murky arena. With that said, here are a few approaches to consider or avoid that may help you get your foot in the door.

PART 1: RESEARCH

The number one piece of advice offered by music supervisors on panels everywhere: do your homework. Doing as much research as possible will not only help you find the right people to contact but ensure you don't waste their time – or yours.

Know Who You're Pitching

Don't just send out a blind press release or blast every person remotely connected with film or TV music whose email you are able to track down. Know whom you are reaching out to and their role in placing music in media. The following is a road map of some of the key players in this process.

Third Party Pitching Companies

The primary function of these companies or people (a/k/a "sync agents") is pitching and placing music in media. They do not handle your publishing, put out records or construct your marketing campaign (though there are some that do offer ancillary services including those just mentioned). Most "administer" certain rights for a percentage of the sync fee. These deals will be explored further in the last chapter, but for now the important detail to note is that these companies are neither traditional publishers (e.g. Kobalt, Warner/Chappell Music Publishing) nor labels (Sony, Warner Brothers Records). These should be number one on your music licensing "hit list", over labels, publishers or even music supervisors. It will be more beneficial in the long run to try to gain representation by a pitching company rather than cold call a big studio or an independent supervisor for several reasons:

1. It allows you as an artist to spend more time creating music rather than organizing paperwork and sending emails.

2. Many music supervisors and music supervision companies do not take any unsolicited material. The only way for your music to get through this barrier is via an established source.

3. Studios and music supervisors get so many calls and emails everyday, it's easy for an unknown artist (or pitching company) to get lost in the shuffle. If an album is sent from a company or person whose tastes I know (and like), chances are good it will be moved to the front of the list.

4. Pitching companies have relationships with music supervisors, music executives and so forth already in place. They know how each person likes to receive music and how each likes to be approached.

5. The most important element of a pre-existing relationship between a pitching company and a music supervisor is trust. If a reputable pitching company sends a song it is understood that they have already vetted it for any potential clearance pitfalls so there is a low risk of issues arising down the line. Every music supervisor has been burned at least once in a situation where the person sending the music was not properly educated and a deal was botched. These tales are told at gatherings over a bottle (bottles) of wine like ghost stories around a campfire. A song pitched to a project for a very limited budget has a surprise third writer signed to a major publisher. A licensor claims they own 100% of both the master recording and publishing, and it turns out to be an obscure cover. In the worst-case scenario, this can lose a client and a paycheck. Therefore, it

should be no surprise that trusting collaborators is of the utmost importance.

The moral of the story: your music is more likely to be moved to the top of the bin if it comes from someone a music supervisor already knows, respects and trusts.

Of course, there are hundreds of such companies. There are those like Crucial Music, Songtradr and 411 Music Group with large searchable databases, and others that are more boutique like Lip Sync Music, Ghost Town, The Greater Goods Co. and Secret Road Music Services...and hundreds more all of which have their own specialties, strengths and deal structures. Where do you even start?

First target representation by pitching companies who have a strong catalog where you feel your music would fit best. This will go a long way in putting your music directly on a music supervisor's radar. For example, if you are a hip-hop artist, you don't want to be represented by a company with a reputation for primarily having a catalog of singer-songwriters. Chances are a music supervisor won't have that company top of mind when they are seeking hip-hop. Conversely, if a company has too much music too similar to yours, you may get lost in the shuffle. If your specialty is writing and performing pop in the vein of Katy Perry and you come across a company who has great pop music - but only like Grimes or Lady Gaga, you may complement and add depth to their roster. Tips for finding such companies will be discussed shortly. You can be sure though, that all of them will appreciate the same submission parameters as those outlined for music supervisors in later chapters, starting with doing your research.

A subset of such companies is a **Music Library** (a/k/a Production Music Library). These are enormous catalogs containing thousands of mostly instrumental tracks, though now many are signing deals with artists as well. If you are a "jack of all trades" musician (e.g. composer, song-writer, artist, etc.) a music library may be a good fit. Licensing from them is usually less expensive than licensing from labels, publishers and third-party pitching companies. In film and scripted television, music supervisors usually go to music libraries for specialty needs such as cocktail jazz in the background of a lounge, elevator muzak, etc. – in unscripted television, however, an entire series might be scored with cues from music libraries. As with other pitching companies, each music library has a specialty or genres at which it excels. De Wolfe Music, for example, has a huge catalog of authentic vintage music from the early 1900s up to today. Other companies that fall into this category include APM Music, Extreme Music, FirstCom Music, Killer Tracks, Megatrax and West One Music Group.

Music Supervisors

Again, music supervisors are exponentially more likely to pay attention to your music if it comes from someone they trust. So much music comes in every day that prioritization is essential. There are still some who do listen to artist submissions, but per any number of the reasons listed above, don't be offended if your email goes unanswered.

Often working alongside music supervisors are **music coordinators**. The role of a music coordinator can vary widely from person to person, company to company, but generally they act as the right hand to the music supervisor. While a music supervisor is responsible for overseeing and executing the "big picture" of all things relating to music on a project (liaising with the director or showrunner, producers, studio, etc.) a music coordinator often handles the nitty gritty – tracking shooting schedules, script changes, song research and assisting with the creative, including listening to new artists and music submissions that come in. Often music coordinators are the "next generation" of music supervisors in training, so you'd be well advised not to ignore them to get to the bigger name.

Studio Music Executives

It's not completely unfruitful to reach out to these people. When it comes to studio films (a/k/a "the big money"), they might have more decision-making power than independent music supervisors, and can have their hands in more projects at any given time. Plus every music professional - studio executive or independent music supervisor - wants to be as current with their tastes and knowledge as possible. Their wider role at the studio, however, means that studio executives aren't usually in the trenches when it comes to pitching songs, initiating music searches and so forth. They may even have a stricter "no unsolicited submissions" policy than an independent music supervisor.

Content Creators (**Producers, Directors, Writers, Editors, Television "Showrunners"**)

For content creators, there are no label, publisher or other music industry politics. Music is still a joyful thing, rather than an aggressive current that one has to fight against daily. They just want to make the best movie or show they can and maybe help out a friend in the process. Befriend them if you have the opportunity, but don't ever try to use these relationships to go above or behind the back of a music supervisor or music executive - it's a quick way to never get a call from them again.

There are of course a myriad of other roles in the creation of a film: editors, music editors, production lawyers and more, all of whom have the potential to influence the music depending on the situation. Pursuing all of them would drive anyone insane, so take the time to really consider the optimal approach both for you and the music supervisors on the other end. Take heed though, it's not wise to send a blast to every email address or Twitter handle you can find. While many, many hopeful artists do take this approach... emails, Tweets and Facebook messages that were clearly copied, pasted and carelessly fired off to everyone are not a good idea. This approach is often first on the list of reasons a music supervisor will delete a cold email.

Know What You're Pitching For

So how do you figure out whom to target? It's an uphill battle to try to fit a square peg in a round hole, so start by asking yourself:

Who are the people and companies working on the projects that are the best fit for my music?

Answering this question will take time and perseverance. Fortunately, there are a variety of different strategies and resources available that will provide you all the information needed, especially if you are willing to do a little digging. This work will pay off in a big way so I encourage you to do so.

Start with the fun part: **consume content.** Watch television, movies, trailers, advertisements, video games, etc. Pay attention to the music and sound and feel of the programming you watch and learn who the typical audience is that watches it. Compare that with the music you have to offer and decide if it honestly fits. If you have electronic dance music, think about the types of shows and movies that might use that. As you pay more attention to the music used in what you watch, you'll get a better feel for what types of music shows most often use. This can apply broadly to television networks as well. MTV has a particular "sound", as does Bravo, Lifetime, Freeform, etc. Alternative sports programming often has upbeat electronic dance music or upbeat rock to match both the pace of what's going on and the audience watching. Primetime family and workplace dramas often favor indie pop and/or acoustic singer songwriters, etc. Make sure to take note not only of the big emotional montages, but the background music, too. Is there a location the characters regularly visit, like a coffee shop or bar? There might only be one featured music moment in an episode (or less) but five, six or seven songs playing at the dive bar.

Television is often an easier medium to assess because you'll likely have some existing shows in mind that you'd like to pitch for. With film, it's important to know what's in development or production, which isn't something you can just turn on the TV to find out (except for some entertainment news programming). Advertisements and trailers are the most secretive and difficult to find information on. Here are some of the websites and publications music supervisors and executives alike turn to for their news:

- Variety (Website or print version)
- The Hollywood Reporter (Website or print version)
- Deadline
- IndieWire
- The Wrap
- Cinemablend
- Ad Age
- Billboard
- Music Business Worldwide
- MusicWeek

I also advise following these sites and their writers on Twitter for the most breaking news.

By investing in this type of research not only will you gain an understanding of the type of content (genre, style, budget, medium) your music may have a home in, but also a direction to pursue when utilizing the following tools.

IMDb – Internet Movie Database

If you're not already familiar with this website you have some work to do. IMDb is a database detailing TV, film and online content along with the cast and below-the-line crew (a/k/a the off-screen players). While not always 100% reliable, IMDb can inform you as to who the music supervisor on a project is, what else they may currently be working on and what they've done in the past. For a fee, there is also IMDbPRO, which will provide more comprehensive information and details for projects in pre-production as well as contact information for Production Companies and more.

Start with a film (or television show) you love or you believe would have been a great fit for your music. Who was the music supervisor? What are they working on now? Scroll down through all of their credits and see if any patterns emerge. Does this music supervisor work on mostly family films? Does that one work on edgy TV comedies?

IMDb is also one of the only places to list end credits for all the songs used in a film on the Soundtracks page, including songs used from pitching companies and music libraries. The names of these companies (as well as labels) will usually appear at the end of any of the following phrases: "by arrangement with", "courtesy of", "under license to" and so forth. A quick Google search should be able to bring you to their website and inform you of the type of company they are.

A hearty warning though: IMDb is not a perfect system. It is not always correct or up to date. While it is a very helpful resource, it should not be treated as the one and only Truth.

TuneFind

There are several websites that provide information on which artists and songs are used in television shows and films, but TuneFind is the most reputable and comprehensive. While much of the data is crowd-sourced, many music supervisors have accounts and provide the information directly to the website. Like IMDb, TuneFind will also include songs used from music libraries and lesser-known third-party pitching companies. Some pages will also tell you who the show's music supervisor is as well. Again since it's mainly user-generated content, some details can be missing or inaccurate. Also, some shows do change their sound from season to season (e.g. *American Horror Story*), so do not assume that last season's needs are the same as this season. Still, it is a great tool to use in tandem with IMDb and other websites.

The Guild of Music Supervisors

This website is a good place to get familiar with some of the names in the Music Supervision world which you can then look up on IMDb to see what they've been up to. Every year the GMS presents the annual Guild of Music Supervisors Awards and State of Music in Media Conference, which are inclusive of music supervisors across all media (film, television, trailers, advertising and brands).

The Music Business Registry - Film & Television Music Guide

A book and digital registry updated several times a year containing contact information for music supervisors, production company music departments, film studio music departments, TV network music departments, music editors actually editing the music placed in TV/Film, record label and publishing company TV/Film departments and more. It's the most convenient solution but also the most expensive. Please use this information with discretion as music supervisors tend to find that when contact information winds up in here, it results in a deluge of unsolicited submissions, making many less likely to listen to anything that comes in. The information in Chapter 4 will help guide you on what music to consider pitching and when.

. . .

Film and Music Conferences

A few of these were already mentioned in the last chapter. Every year there are dozens of music and film conferences around the world, and many include panels on topics related to music licensing. As an emerging artist or pitching company it is worth attending at least a few of these for a myriad of reasons, but one is to gain insight into the needs of (and hopefully meeting) music supervisors, label representatives, pitching company owners, publishers, music executives and so forth. Even if you cannot attend due to distance or the event being limited to organization members only, the websites alone will provide a wealth of knowledge through panelist or speaker biographies, press coverage listing participating speakers and companies, and sometimes even overviews or recordings of the panels.

Here are a few conferences that frequently feature panels on music supervision and licensing:

- South by Southwest (SXSW) Music Conference (Austin, TX)
- Nashville Film Festival (Nashville, TN)
- ASCAP I Create Music EXPO (Los Angeles, CA)
- Durango Songwriters Expo (Ventura & Santa Ynez, CA and Durango, CO)
- MUSEXPO (Los Angeles, CA)
- Guild Of Music Supervisors State of Music in Media Conference (Los Angeles, CA)

- Canadian Music Week (Toronto, ON)
- Canadian Music Café at TIFF (Toronto, ON)
- Sync Summit (Worldwide)

These events are popping up all over the world. Keep an eye out for any conferences in a town near you!

While the above resources are good places to start, they are by no means the only places. Most music supervisors have personal or company websites which you should visit. Follow them on Twitter. Read biographies, interviews and panel transcripts; find out everything you can about the music supervisors you are pitching to and the shows they work on. Many networks include song lists on the show's page, or feature the music on Twitter, Spotify or other platforms (such as the ABC Music Lounge).

PART 2: TECHNOLOGY

At this time, you are armed with a specific list of companies, music supervisors, and projects to target. In this day and age, there are almost countless ways to connect with people - snail mail, email, phone, texting, Twitter, Facebook, LinkedIn, and the list goes on. While it might seem like the more platforms you use, the greater chance there is of someone them listening to your music, that is often not the case. Using the wrong methods to contact a music supervisor can result in at best being ignored at best and at worst being actively removed from the list of trusted contacts.

1. Email. This is far and away the preferred contact method for most music supervisors. Emails can contain more information than any of the other platforms below (most importantly music) in the most efficient way. They can also be filed and referred to later as needed, essential for a busy music supervisor. Hallmarks of a successful pitch email from tone to technical elements will be discussed further in the next chapter.

2. Snail Mail. Some music supervisors still do prefer to receive physical CDs, particularly for artists they love or if the album artwork is unique. CDs can also be helpful for Los Angeles residents with long commutes. Similarly, USB flash drives are handy (and popular) tools for delivering a large amount of data in a small, neat package, ideal if sending more than one album or a catalog of score cues. That said, many music supervisors toss unsolicited materials directly into the circular so think twice before spending money on physical submissions, and first ask if that is the preferred submission method. Suggested delivery specifications for both CDs and USB flash drives can be found later on in the next chapter.

It is also recommended to send an email in conjunction with snail mail. Sending music via snail mail alone may come across as antiquated. Plus, it is easier for a music supervisor to lose a stray piece of paper with your contact information that may have been taped or attached by rubber band to a CD, than an email.

3. Phone Calls. Speaking of antiquated...Ultimately the approach will almost always depend on the type of relationship and with whom you're dealing. music supervisors that have been in the business for decades have sources that they've used equally as long and are friends with at this point. In those cases, calls are commonplace and are as much a friendly catch up as it is about a pitch. However, please take note that this is an exception from the norm.

Most relationships are more "professional" than the one described above; you've had some correspondence over email and maybe chatted at networking mixers or went out to drinks or lunch. For people in this circle, email is your best bet, especially if you are checking on current needs.

No relationship at all? Definitely do not cold call.

While a phone call may successfully corner a music supervisor into disclosing current music needs, many music supervisors find it easier to provide clearer direction when not put on the spot. Sending a song brief via email or at least being the one to initiate the call ensures time to gather our thoughts, yielding not only a more comprehensive description but also one that can be referenced anytime as needed by either party.

Plus, if there is one thing I've learned from experience and research, it is that most music supervisors are in the middle of several tasks at a time and do not appreciate being pulled away from a pressing assignment to chat with yet another pitching company or independent artist. By using email, you don't interrupt what they're working on, and you leave it to them to read and respond when they're ready as opposed to annoying them.

While most pitching companies favor email, a handful of phone calls still come in every week. To be completely honest, 98% of the pitchers who do phone check-ins these days seem to be those who have been in the business a very long time. It's frankly become a dated practice and it's unlikely that you want music supervisors to perceive you or your catalog as dated.

With that said, there are a few other situations in which picking up the phone is warranted: anything time sensitive or if an explanation is just too complicated to type.

Similarly, do not call someone's cell phone unless absolutely necessary (e.g. you're working on an urgent clearance for them and they are out of the office). To be clear, it is not an urgent situation if they simply haven't responded to your email about your latest signing.

If you just do a little bit of digging, you'll probably find an email address somewhere.

4. Text Messaging. Unless you are personal friends, *texting with a music supervisor client is not appropriate.* Have they invited you to their birthday party? If not, they probably don't consider you a personal friend. The only exception to this rule is if a music supervisor initiated the text conversation or specifically asked that you text them about something e.g. an urgent clearance. Nearly everyone

I polled feels that this is a violation of common courtesy (and personal space).

5. LinkedIn, Facebook and Twitter - There are always exceptions, however the majority of music supervisor colleagues do not accept music submissions via social media platforms. It is impossible to demonstrate you did your research and are knowledgeable about music clearance in an 140-character tweet, and tweeting at us asking for current needs or how to submit music is extremely lazy. Many music supervisors use Facebook for personal purposes only.

If you absolutely cannot find an email address anywhere, a Facebook message may be considered if it is treated as email (rather than a chat tool). However don't friend anyone you haven't already corresponded with via email or haven't met face to face. Though LinkedIn is the most business-oriented social media platform, very few creative music professionals use it actively. It is much more popular (and in fact, necessary) in other professions. The only exception to this rule is if you come across a call for music submissions via one of these platforms and the initiating music supervisor does not provide an email.

PART 3: ETIQUETTE

Hopefully you have now been convinced to reach out via email to a specially curated list of music supervisors. What do you say in the email? How are you supposed to stand out and convince someone to respond?

The specific components of a good pitch email will be broken down shortly, but none of that will matter if your overall tone is rude, pushy, arrogant or flippant. To begin, here are some etiquette tips to inform your overall approach. Keep these in mind for every interaction from email to phone calls and even in person.

1. Be professional. Whether an intern or executive, it's incredible how often people forget that the music business is still "business." When first approaching a music supervisor, treat the interaction as you would a job interview. Would you wear faded jeans and an old t-shirt to meet a prospective employer? No! Though many clearly think the opposite, this type of attire is not appropriate for any interview, including an entry-level gig in music. That however, is for another book. Seriously though, would you give a recruiter or your potential future boss a big hug upon meeting them? Definitely not.

Yes, the goal is to build a comfortable rapport with a music supervisor, pitching company or studio executive. It's important to understand though that to do so successfully can take time. Don't come in too hot, too aggressive and/or too personal.

Even if you are a super friendly, happy and open person, it's essential to respect that the person you are reaching out to may not be the same. Forcing a friendship almost always comes across insincere.

It's incredibly difficult to gauge someone's personality - and sense of humor - from an email exchange. Don't try to be extra funny or kitschy thinking that will immediately endear you to someone. They will remember you, but it may not be for a good reason. To this point, below are several elements to leave out of early exchanges. Wait until your prospective client introduces any of the following before broaching yourself:

- Personal terms of endearment such as: honey, lady, girl, dude, man, sweetie
- Slang words or phrases
- Personal details about yourself or the person you are emailing, including kids, spouses, hometowns, weekend or vacation plans, or recent illnesses. Mentioning family is one thing, opening a professional email with a paragraph about a trip to the zoo gone awry is different.
- Emoticons, especially the winking smiley face
- Sarcasm

Be wary of going too far the other direction as well. While it's understood music blasts of new albums, singles, samplers and so forth are sent to mailing lists of fellow music supervisors, it is important that introductory emails not look like they have been sent from a mailbot. Rather than asking "what up dude?" personalize the email by being clear it was written specifically for the reader (more on that shortly).

2. Be humble. More specifically, tread lightly on the fine line between being confident and presumptuous. The goal is to convince the person you are emailing to do business with you, to listen to your music and reach out to you when they are in need of song ideas. To that end, it is important to convey that you are smart, savvy, dependable, talented and can provide good music; you're someone they want to be in business with.

Of course, you cannot say that outright as written above (though many do). Doing so tends to make music supervisors think the opposite. The challenge is finding ways to communicate the same information without coming across boastful or smug. Remember: good music and good service speaks for itself.

Below are few phrases submitted by a selection of fellow music supervisors that make them cringe (and are heard far too often):

- I have the perfect song for you!
- I have exactly what you have been looking for!
- You need to listen to this right now!
- This will be the best [song, album, artist] you have heard all week.
- This [song, album, artist] will change your life, I guarantee it.
- I'm confident this song would be a great fit for X show.

3. Use proper grammar, spelling, punctuation and sentence structure. This may seem obvious, but it is not. I have gotten many a cold email from music producers as follows:

"Hi. I want to put music into your soundtracks. Let me know what your working on!!!!!!!"

Possibly in an effort to "personalize" emails or because the music industry seems more lax than others, people often seem to throw out the rulebook on proper grammar. This only makes the writer (and any company associated) appear unprofessional or even dimwitted. Seek out ways to inject personality into an email while still demonstrating you have a respectable grasp of the English language.

4. Be efficient. Try to get across essential information in as few words as possible. Think of it this way: if you were at a corporate office job, you wouldn't post up in your boss's office waxing poetic about your recent trip to Paris unless he or she actually asked, "How are you? How was your trip to Paris?" Imagine you are working for the music supervisor, rather than trying to get them to do you a favor by listening to and/or placing your music.

This applies to personal interactions as well as emails. If you were to meet a music supervisor at an industry mixer during the ASCAP I Create Music Expo, they will be more impressed if you keep the conversation brief and as little about your catalog as possible. Be personable and sincere; make your point and then move on. End the conversation by asking for an email address or passing them your card and send the full spiel after the fact.

One more note on meeting etiquette

While the advice in this chapter applies to in-person meetings as well, there is one additional tip that new pitchers or artists meeting with music supervisors should note. *If you have requested a meeting with a music supervisor, be prepared to pay.* If that sounds entitled, I didn't make it up. The same concept extends beyond the music industry to essentially every field of business, networking drinks, informational interviews, etc. If you are at a company, you likely have an expense account to cover this (if not, ask for one). As a starving artist though, it's completely understood that you're not in a position to suggest a dinner at Mozza. Please don't break the bank! By all means suggest a place yourself to have some control over the costs. However, if you've asked for a coffee meeting and do not at least offer to purchase their coffee (or tea, or juice) it marks you as an amateur. Meeting at their office? Offer to bring coffee, or lunch if it's lunchtime. They may decline, but it is always professional and savvy to do so.

4 THE FIRST PITCH

Now that you know how to *approach* the initial email, what do you actually *write*? Unfortunately, there is no such thing as the "perfect" pitch. No music delivery method that is preferred by all music supervisors. No tactic or strategy that every single person loves and will guarantee a response. There are, however, certain gripes, frustrations and predilections that are shared by many of us. While bad grammar and an inappropriate tone are certainly among these, there are still more landmines to avoid...as well as gold-star techniques to employ that, at the very least, will demonstrate you did your homework, one thing that every music supervisor appreciates.

While some of these grievances have been addressed in a macro way, this chapter will break down a "good" pitch email section by section.

THE INTRODUCTION

As mentioned in the previous chapter, music supervisors can tell right away when they are getting a blast email even if the first line is "Hi Peter." You should include both their name and a detail that makes it clear you took the time to write to them individually, like mentioning specific projects your research indicates they may be working on (or have worked on in the past) or even just projects of theirs that you admire. Most music supervisors are far more likely to respond to an email that shows intention and research than a mailbot.

That said, at some point in your career you will most likely send out a blast email to established (not new) contacts, especially if your catalog grows large enough. When that time comes make sure to blind copy (or "bcc") all recipients. The blind copy hides all email addresses the note is being sent to thereby protecting the privacy of all included. Even though many of us do know each other, privacy is extremely important to music supervisors. Forgetting to "bcc" is widely considered an amateur move or embarrassing mistake.

THE PITCH

Music supervisors get cold emails from new artists, pitching companies, labels and publishing companies every day, often more than one per day. So many that the only way to stay sane is to come to terms with the fact that there is simply no way to keep up with it all (at least not in a timely manner).

Many peers have said that a lengthy email will cause them to either delete or skim, daunted by the block of text. While there is a great deal of information to cover, remember to try and keep it as concise as possible. Try to break up large paragraphs into a few sentences each.

You have already been warned that being overly kitschy, sassy or cute are not effective ways to get attention. Remember: professional and personable. Now onward to a few suggestions on how to best to deploy this knowledge.

1. Start with a brief overview of your company and/or who you are. What is your relationship to the music being pitched? Are you the founder or president of the company? Main composer? Lead singer? Manager? Do you represent all the publishing, a portion of the publishing, the master recordings or both? Be clear about the type of company you are whether it's publicity, management, a publisher, label, third party pitching company or a hybrid of one of more of those.

If you are not the direct contact for clearing the songs you are sending – for example, a manager whose client is signed to a label and publisher and whose songs often have many co-writers – please include this information somewhere in the email and make sure the correct clearance contacts are in the metadata of the tracks sent. While it's understandable that you want to help facilitate the process and having direct access to an artist is often helpful, being given the actual clearance contacts up front rather than having to go through you to get them saves time.

If you are the artist, include any current or exciting news (e.g. new EP release, on tour with Taylor Swift, just won *The Voice*), social media statistics and maybe even one or two links to articles and reviews by notable publications – Billboard counts, your friend's personal blog does not. Still, be prepared for many music supervisors not to care about these things. Most of the time, Twitter followers won't have any effect on a placement – if a song really works (or doesn't work) in a scene, that information is irrelevant. However, in a situation where a placement comes down to your song and that of another artist without any "story" around them as the final two contenders, both enhancing the moment equally well, it's likely the music supervisor will go with the more "buzzing" artist in the hopes that buzz will help market the show.

2. Demonstrate you have an understanding of the music licensing process. As mentioned earlier, a major reason why music supervisors can be hesitant to work with new companies and artists is the fear of being burned by ineptitude. You need to allay these fears right off the bat.

Make sure you are very familiar with the clearance process detailed in Chapter 1. Sync, all in, pro-rata, MFN, publishing, masters, PRO, one stop...these are just a few of the common terms used in music placement and licensing that you should understand and feel confident using. Take the time to get comfortable with the lingo, because not knowing the language will strike fear (or at least suspicion) in the hearts of many music supervisors.

Since the clearance process can happen very quickly, offering (and delivering) fast service and a quick ("easy") turnaround on clearances will be music to a music supervisor's ears. Add "affordable" to the mix and you're on your way.

Many companies and artists, however, already have all of that down. At least two thirds of all emails from third party pitching companies promise an "affordable, easy clear and/or 100% one stop catalog covering all genres." Defining yourself or your company by those attributes alone is simply not enough.

3. Highlight what makes you different from the rest. Why should I send a music search to you over all the other easy-clear, one-stop companies that have high-quality music of all genres? Do you represent any major or notable emerging artists? Are there any genres you specialize in?

The desire to avoid boxing yourself in is completely understandable; as a library or pitching company you want to be able to service any and all needs to keep the business going! True, there may not be as many searches for 1960's French pop music as frequently as indie rock. However, I don't always go to every company that has indie rock when that need arises – in fact, that *rarely* happens, if ever. That one genre alone would cover dozens companies and I'd be downloading submissions for a week. Stake your claim as a specialist, and you will be the first phone call every time a need arises for 1960's French pop music or authentic Jamaican steel drum tunes.

THE MUSIC

You may be tempted to follow up your mission statement by asking about current projects or what music you can send to make their day brighter. Avoid doing this. Many music supervisors say they hate the phrases, "Do you need music?" "What are you working on?" or "Can I send you some music?" In those situations, it's less time consuming to reply with, "I'm good at the moment but thanks!" than to explain the programs and placement opportunities. That being said, in certain media like trailers or advertising, it's almost impossible to know what someone is working on (there is no IMDb for trailers) so, "What are your needs?" is a bit more welcome. Even so, asking if you can send music before sending anything may seem respectful, but is actually creating more work. Though brief, responding "Yes you can" is another item on the to do list. Just send the music in the initial email.

What Music Do I Send?

It is likely that you have a long list of songs or artists you want to get into the hands of a music supervisor. What if the song(s) you *don't* send are actually the exact songs perfect for their projects? While this is a logical fear, resist the urge to send a link to your entire catalog in this first email.

Be selective and try to limit yourself to 7- 10 tracks. Consider this: the more music you send, the greater the chance your folder of songs will get passed over. With that in mind, there are two approaches to consider:

The Best of Sampler

Think of this as a snapshot of your strengths. It should support the written overview of your company above and include notable songs, artists and genres you believe make your catalog strong and unique.

A Project Sampler

A selection of songs chosen with the project(s) of the supervisor in mind.

You've done your research, so you have some idea of what the music supervisor you are emailing may be working on or has worked on in the past. Take a moment and think:

"Does my music really fit into anything they're working on?"

If you really do believe your music could potentially work for a music supervisor's projects (be honest with yourself) then assemble a playlist of songs with that project in mind. Maybe it's some moody singer-songwriters for *The Vampire Diaries*, or hip hop for *Empire* or epic orchestral music for a trailer music supervisor. However, this is a balancing act. No matter how much research you have done, avoid acting as though you know their music needs as well or better than they do. Simply present your ideas and then offer to create a playlist in a different direction if these are not in line with the project's creative vision. They probably won't be, but every music supervisor I know appreciates the effort put into a respectful and educated attempt over the blind pitch approach.

If your music really doesn't fit into any of their current project you have two options:

1. Wait. Spend your time and energy only pitching music supervisors who are working on projects appropriate for your music. Circle back to the others only if and when you notice they sign on to a project with a sound more in line with what you have to offer. We've heard music supervisors state that they simply delete emails that don't pertain to their current needs, so a targeted approach is ideal if your time is limited.

2. Send a best of sampler as detailed above. You never know when the right opportunity will arise, and your music will be perfect. The key part of this exchange, however, is being clear that you are aware there may not be a need for your music at the moment. Should they ever be seeking some good quality dirty rap (for example) though, you're ready. And then, only send a few of your cleanest tracks (both in terms of expletives and subject matter).

The optimal strategy is a combination of these two approaches – best of and project-based. Keep in mind, in this initial interaction it is most important to showcase the music that really makes you as an artist or company, great. Don't send mediocre tracks in an attempt to prove your catalog has depth or to meet a project need you aren't even sure about.

Of course, you don't need to be told that music is subjective. "Pop" or "Upbeat" can mean different sounds to different ears (and minds). Are you unsure what tracks best represent your music or that could fit in a commercial romantic comedy? Seek second opinions from trusted friends, colleagues, mentors or collaborators and really listen to their feedback.

How Should I Send My Music?

You are already well aware of the importance of metadata, but now to get into the technical nitty-gritty of actually delivering the music. This is one of the most frequently asked questions during panels. Preferences will vary, so prepare for the inevitability that at least a couple music supervisors will request a different format. Following the advice below, however, will go a long way in demonstrating you have put thought into the process.

1. Never send files as attachments. They take up valuable inbox real estate and consequently can cause email functions to come grinding to a halt. No one likes this. In fact, some music supervisors (and publishers, labels and pitching companies) will delete any emails with attachments before reading a single word.

2. Provide both streaming and downloading options. This way, the receiver can preview tracks by streaming and download only those that tickle their fancy.

If you only provide a download option, they may pass over your email (too busy to download, reading your email on their cell phone, slow internet connection, etc.)

Dropbox, Hightail (formerly Yousendit), WeTransfer and Box are all acceptable services to use to send files. Everyone has a different preference, but many like Box because you can easily stream *and* download tracks either individually or in bulk. SoundCloud is a great service for streaming, but until they allow you to download all songs in a Set at once, make sure to include a link to download all tracks in one click (or two) as well. That said, we have heard from those at pitching companies that SoundCloud and Bandcamp's comprehensive interfaces can be helpful for their submission process since an artist's SoundCloud profile can include contact information, social media handles and more.

There are also services like Songspace, DISCO, Synch-Tank and Source Audio, which are designed specifically for delivering music, and many pitching companies large and small use them. DISCO, in particular, is becoming an industry norm and as favored as (if not more than) Box.

Regardless of which one you choose, take time to learn how to properly utilize these services. Not doing so is a fast way to seem like an amateur. For example, Dropbox and Box both have functions enabling users to share folders with others; in this scenario the shared folder appears in each user's account indefinitely. In the case of some services, like Dropbox, shared folders consume storage space in both the sender and recipient's accounts, other services like Box take up only visual space, with the files themselves stored only in the sender's account. Shared folders also yield extra emails, further cluttering an already full inbox. Instead, copy and paste a **shared link** to your playlist into the body of your email, a function fairly intuitive in all of the services listed above.

3. Aim for as few clicks as possible. Yes, I know that if I go to your band's website and follow the hyperlinks to your Bandpage or SoundCloud profile, I can listen to music. Unfortunately though many music supervisors won't take that time for a band they have never heard of (there are antsy editors and producers who need to be serviced ASAP!) With music submissions constantly flooding in, the fewer clicks or steps to access what you're pitching the better.

To this point, it is important to consider the different ways someone might want to ingest your music and plan accordingly.

Sending three albums? First of all, only do this if you are specifically asked or if you are actively releasing new songs or albums every week. Then, make sure there are links to download each album individually as well as one to download all three together.

Sending a sampler? It's possible someone might only want one artist or song out of the bunch. Box is great for this since the listener can stream and download individual tracks as well as the whole folder.

No matter how many individual artists, tracks or albums you may be showcasing in the email, always include a link to "download all" somewhere easily accessible. Even if you are only sending three songs make sure to provide a link where all three can be downloaded at once.

4. Always send MP3s, but make high-quality versions (like WAV or AIF) available as well. Large files can clog up a hard drive the same way audio attachments can clog up an email inbox. Most music supervisors initially work with MP3s (ideally 320 kbps) and then request higher quality files once we are approaching the final mix. That said, some do prefer the higher audio quality of WAV or AIF files, and one never knows when a last-minute request for a WAV will arise. It is always preferable to not to have to reach out to a third party when time is of the essence. If you do include WAV or AIF files, organize them in a way that the MP3s alone can be easily downloaded (i.e. put the high-quality versions in a separate folder). Once again, keep in mind MP3, M4A and AIF files can carry meta-data, WAVs cannot.

5. Don't send links that expire. What you pitch might not be appropriate for a music supervisor's projects right now, but what about six weeks from now? What about a year? Many peers regularly file emails for future reference. Currently they may only be searching for urban and pop music. Six months later they may begin work on a television show using entirely Americana and folk. The first stop is usually to the email folder, searching for those genre keywords.

If that link is expired and cannot be accessed weeks or months later, there's a good chance they'll move on to other options. The hard truth that is there is just so much music available, it's more efficient to move onto the next rather than spend time tracking down a new link. Personally I regularly revisit emails and links sent more than a year ago.

6. Offer alternate submission methods. While email is far and away the most popular way to send music, it's also a good idea to offer physical submissions as well - some music supervisors do still prefer this method to digital links.

If you are sending music via "snail mail" on CD or flash drive, here are some tips to consider when assembling your package.

DELIVERING VIA CD

Disc Format

Data or MP3 CDs are almost always preferable to Audio CDs as you can fit more tracks on one disc, and when importing into iTunes all the metadata remains in the track. There is nothing more frustrating than popping a CD into the computer and having "Track 1, Track 2..." show up. That said, many people get some of their best listening done while in the car and not every car is MP3 CD compatible.

If you are sending physical music to a music supervisor for the first time, send one Audio and one Data CD of your introductory "best of" sampler and your most recent release to make sure your bases are covered. It is also possible to submit track info for a burned CD to Gracenote via iTunes. Searching the Internet will provide a few different sets of instructions for this process.

Packaging and Appearance

Always print out the track list and insert it into the jewel case (iTunes makes this very easy). Printing it directly onto the CD is fine, but if you've sent an Audio CD (Track 1, Track 2...), and that is the only place to find song titles and artist names...you've made it significantly harder for your client to enter the information into their music library.

The CD packaging should be polished and professional. While full press kits, glossy photos and similar trimmings are a waste of money - at least as music supervisors are concerned - the CD casing and artwork should look professional. Do not send a burned disc with the album title written on in Sharpie.

Also, ensure your contact information is securely attached to the CD itself. A one-sheet with a bio, description and any other marketing details about the band can be helpful, but contact information is essential. Make sure it cannot get accidentally tossed into the trash, leaving a naked, stray

CD. To stress again, if a music supervisor cannot figure out where a song came from, they cannot clear it and cannot use it. Eliminate any confusion by printing your name, company (if applicable) and email and sticking it directly onto the CD cover *and* CD itself.

DELIVERING VIA FLASH DRIVE

Flash drives are typically used to send large quantities of music and are helpful if a music supervisor requests your entire catalog. Plus, as less and less computers have disc drives, all of them have USB ports. If you are sending a large (or even medium) quantity of music, make sure the files are organized by artist or genre instead of a single folder of eighty tracks. Double-check that all your track metadata is up to date. It is also a good idea to include a "best of" sampler or playlist geared to their projects as well.

SIGNING OFF

When wrapping up your email be gracious and accommodating first and foremost. Asking how often you can check in or send music is perfectly fine. Thank them for their consideration and for listening to the music. That is all you need to do.

Unfortunately, more often than not, people take an unnecessary step further. While none of the following requests are considered offensive, be prepared for them to go unanswered (and here's why)...

1. Don't ask to set up a call or meeting to discuss further. Offering it as an option should the music supervisor be interested is one thing (and totally fine), but requesting times or availability for a call to discuss your music further assumes they have that time to spare and many music supervisors don't. If you have music that is relevant to their current needs, they will be calling you.

2. Don't ask to be on the brief list. Pitchers often ask to be added to "search lists" or "blast lists," which are broadly defined as email distribution or group lists some music supervisors use when sending out music searches for specific needs. In truth, most music supervisors do not have one blast list, and if they do, it is comprised of people who have proven themselves to be a trusted source - not those they have never done business with. I don't know a single music supervisor who adds a company to a list simply because they asked. And whether they asked or not, if I added every person, artist or company to a single list, I would be downloading music for months after every search and respectively unable to do the majority of the job that does not involve listening to music. A savvier approach would be to ask to be considered for future searches (or creative briefs, etc.) or to "be on the radar" should the right opportunity arise.

3. Don't ask for feedback. Music supervisors are primarily focused on finding music that fits whatever projects they are working on at the moment. If your music meets that need, you will hear from us. You may get a shout if your music touches us on a personal level as well. We are music fans after all! But if you're looking for actual constructive criticism on how "sync-able" a song might be or specific notes on how closely it fit the creative target (or not)...don't expect an answer. It's never personal and usually a matter of not having the time. Imagine someone handed you their book and asked, "I'd love a book report!" Of course, that's hyperbole - a song is not as long as a book - but you get the idea.

If you do truly want feedback from a music supervisor, look into one of the conferences previously mentioned. NARIP, in particular, hosts events around the world for specifically for artists and songwriters to get feedback on their music.

THE FOLLOW UP

I've sat on many panels where fellow music supervisors have declared, "Never follow up!" and have been known to say the same myself. At the end of the day, if a music supervisor likes and/or wants to use your music, please trust that they will reach out to you...assuming you didn't forget to include your contact information in the metadata of the tracks sent.

That said, you are still a business (or working for one), and lack of persistence is not a great quality in a sales person. Following up is an understandable strategy and you wouldn't be alone in deploying it. Tread carefully though -

while again there is no exact method, keeping the below guidelines in mind will put you ahead of the curve.

1. Wait at least a month after sending the first email. Please don't fire off a, "Checking in to make sure you got this email" follow up within a week. Now that you know just how many music submission emails music supervisors receive every day (again, hundreds) this should make sense. It can take quite a while to get around to listening or responding, even when not solely focused on specific project needs.

2. Don't call. A follow up call might be even worse than the cold call. Either they haven't listened to your music yet (see above regarding the sheer quantity of emails coming in) or they have and just don't have an opportunity at the moment. Regardless, a call is a waste of time for both parties and puts the music supervisor on the spot, undesirable in any scenario.

3. Don't ask if they've had a chance to listen. Assuming your music has been listened to and organized accordingly...if I responded to every person who sent music it would take hours each day. Once again, if an opportunity arises to use a song, you will be contacted.

4. Don't ask for thoughts or feedback. This bears repeating since artists will often use the question as follow up email fluff: "Really excited to know what you think!" or "Just checking in! It would mean so much if you could provide feedback!"

5. Don't be annoyed or passive aggressive.
Sometimes people will call us out for either not responding or not downloading a link in a timely manner. It will leave a bad taste a music supervisor's mouth every time.

If you have sent a carefully crafted introductory email and have only received radio silence in return, try this approach, "I reached out a couple months ago to introduce you to my catalog. The initial email and link to music is below again for your convenience. I wanted to check if it was okay to send you new music going forward?" Obviously, use your own words but you get the idea. Rather than chasing a response to a single piece of music or reel, show that you are a creative force and continue to wow us with your work.

And Then What?

If a music supervisor ignores your emails or won't take the meeting you've requested three times over the past year, don't bang the door down. Don't barrage them with weekly calls or emails. Try a new angle. Do you have mutual friends? Can someone who can vouch for you or your catalog run an introduction? Again, most music supervisors and music executives will prioritize someone recommended by a trusted source. Be patient in these interactions as well, as you certainly don't want to push away a current contact in favor of a making a new one. Introductions can be tricky in every industry; defer to your contact on how comfortable they are making the introduction. Most times when people aren't comfortable with an introduction, it's less about you and more about your contact's relationship with the person you want to meet. You might see that the person you know and the person you want to know are friends on Facebook, but it's possible they haven't spoken in three years. Even if an introduction isn't possible, maybe you'll happen to meet a music supervisor (or a willing connector) at a show or an industry function.

If none of the above tactics are an option, try to limit check-in emails to once a month or every six weeks. As for submitting more music, music supervisors generally want new releases in a timely manner (particularly by notable artists). Try to avoid firing off new tracks willy-nilly every few days though, as those can easily become white noise and get lost in the shuffle. More than one email a week, even of new music, is often considered too much.

When it comes to exposing older tracks in your catalog, stick to once a month. Themed samplers - garage rock, songs about home, montage songs - are a great idea and can be extremely helpful, but don't send them more than once a week, especially if none of the tracks are new.

Whatever avenue you take, if you appear desperate, then a music supervisor might assume it's because you're not getting a lot of business, and then wonder why that is...Be cool. Think of forming a relationship with a music supervisor as courting a potential partner. Give them a summary of what you're about, slip them your number, then give them some space. If they're interested they will come to you.

Then it finally happens. A music supervisor responds, perhaps just complimenting the music sent or expressing thanks. How do you take advantage of the opportunity in a way that keeps the conversation going and growing?

One thing not to do? Don't see it as your window to start a long back and forth email "conversation" and ask even more questions - business or personal (e.g. "Glad you liked it! Do you have any needs today?") If you receive a response from a music supervisor, the best thing to do is thank them for listening, remind them you are there to help and trust that you and your music are on their radar going forward. End the conversation before they do. This applies in social situations as well! And when you do receive a search, knock it out of the park and you will be getting many more emails.

5 HOW TO NAIL A MUSIC SEARCH

Music search. Creative brief. Whatever you call it - artists, pitching companies, labels and publishers all want to find one in their email inbox. Every third cold email from a new company asks to be included on search lists...despite that being somewhat of a fallacy as discussed in the last chapter.

While most music supervisors don't have one "brief list" that they reach out to for every search, many do have a trusted group of "go to" people for certain genres, budgets, types of artists, etc. These are the people who not only have quality music, but more importantly have proven themselves many times over to be savvy and supportive of the music supervision process.

Becoming one of these people often has little to do with whether your song is selected. While striving to meet the creative need is certainly essential, it's extremely difficult to hit a target you cannot see. Respectively, how the music is prepared, packaged and delivered also plays a large role in establishing yourself as a preferred source. Having said that, no one is going to place mediocre music solely because it was submitted properly. Those with truly great music will stand out.

As always, every music supervisor has their own quirks and preferences, so read every part of any search email you receive and make sure to follow any specified delivery requirements. For those music supervisors who are not explicit about their submission preferences, following the parameters outlined in the last chapter (e.g. links that do not expire) coupled with the recommendations below will provide a good starting point.

1. Act Fast. Music searches often require a quick turn-around. If you are an artist and have a label, publisher, administrator or anyone responsible for pitching your music, it's their job to jump on a search the moment it comes in. If you're the one who gets the call - move quickly! Sometimes waiting even five hours before responding can cost you a placement or future searches. There are unfortunately some music supervisors who abuse this, needlessly sending out a call for song ideas at 7pm on Friday night. If you absolutely can't make a specified deadline, definitely feel free to ask if there is flexibility – sometimes there is, sometimes there isn't and sometimes music supervisors encounter a frustrating hybrid of the two! It regularly happens that I'll get a desperate call from an editor needing pre-cleared ideas ASAP and I'll spring into action...only to learn halfway through reaching out to music pitchers that the showrunner just walked in with an idea they are excited about and the fire drill has been called off.

Even if a music supervisor says they don't have a pressing deadline, still try to be as efficient as possible if you can swing it. You never know how many other people are submitting for the same search, and if a music supervisor finds what they need the night before you submit, then your stellar ideas sent the next day may be put on hold before even getting a listen.

Directors and producers also tend to love a song more and more the longer they "live with it" (i.e. see/hear it over and over) in a cut. Sometimes, the plan is to review potential songs for weeks, but then a selection is made in the very first batch sent. The music supervisor can try to present more songs until they are blue in the face, but often when something sticks, it sticks. Bottom line: it's almost always to your advantage to submit music as quickly as possible.

2. Take every reference, keyword or phrase to heart. Yes, you're acting quickly, however, a search that is too creatively off-base will, at best, call into question whether you really cared to deliver or at worst frustrate the recipient for wasting their time. This may seem basic, but if you're given an example of a track to replace, please actually listen to it. Don't just go by the first 10 seconds or referenced artist and assume you understand the need. Is there a percussive break in the middle? Is there a soaring key change? Does it have a button ending or fade out?

A good music supervisor will point out the important details they are seeking to emulate ("The big anthemic build at about 1:00 is really working and I'd love ideas with a similar uplifting change.") Unfortunately, not everyone will. It's easy to see how this would be irritating for those trying meet our needs. Do your best to identify and work off any unique elements throughout the song and when in doubt, feel free to ask for clarification. This is one of the few times a call (rather than email) is deemed appropriate, in the event there are certain details that cannot be put in writing. Once the question is answered, however, avoid steering the conversation into an overall project update and squeezing in the latest news about your roster.

Hopefully you will at least get a scene description along with the reference track. Consider the lyrics in relation to the scene. Even if the search is for low background music in a restaurant during a romantic first date, chances are good that extremely depressing lyrics about heartbreak won't make sense no matter how romantic the tone. If it's a birthday party for a five year old, lyrics about sex or drinking will be inappropriate regardless of how youthful and up-tempo the song.

Keywords are also important. Following a tempo note is important, as it's likely a certain tempo is working with the action of a scene or pace of a montage (if a reference track is included, follow that tempo as a guide). If a music supervisor asks for "authentic" tracks from a time period, they don't want something created last week in a studio, regardless of how authentic it sounds. Unless wiggle room is specifically allowed (sometimes it is), operate as though every descriptive word and adjective has been selected for a reason and aim to check as many boxes as possible when selecting songs to send.

But what if you aren't given any information? Keywords can be subjective!

As mentioned, not every music supervisor writes the most detailed search emails, especially when they are in a rush. Maybe you got a totally bizarre note from a music supervisor that cites an American Authors track as an example of the gritty, dark blues pop they are searching for. You are unsure they have any idea what "blues" or "pop" actually means and the only information about the scene is the name of the show or film. Or, you receive an email that says nothing other than "Need pop like Katy Perry now!" Maybe you've called or emailed in pursuit of clarification and gotten only radio silence (or even more obtuse descriptors) in return.

If you're left totally in the dark, take some time to research everything around the music. If an actor or actress is referenced, look them up. Sometimes seeing the cast can provide a big clue regarding the energy or style of a scene. Watch the trailer for - or even some episodes of - the series (if applicable) to get a sense of the tone. Read the most recent literature on a brand or product and watch other content, commercials, etc. that company has produced. This can be difficult if all that exists for a film is sparse information on an IMDB page, or for a trailer where there is usually no footage of any kind to watch. Still, casting announcements for even the most indie projects can sometimes pop up in Variety or Hollywood Reporter articles. Try looking up past projects from the director or production company.

Do as much as you can to understand the search from every angle and respond accordingly. Is it a network show or family film? If so, chances are good the music supervisor will want clean versions of any tracks with explicit language. If you pick up on such details without us having to point them out, you will be a step ahead of many of your competitors.

3. Only send the best of the best. You may have a ton of sentimental singer songwriter tracks in your catalog, but please don't send all of them. The more focused you can be the better. Most music supervisors would prefer four songs that are totally on point than ten that are kind of close. It's understandable that you want to provide a range to play with, and sometimes music supervisors do wish to be loaded up with music. If a maximum number of tracks is not specified in the search though, assume less is more. You're probably safe sending 7 - 10 tracks. More often than not, opening a folder to find 20+ tracks is a cause for suspicion, and chances are good that more than half the tracks will be closer to B's than A's.

Sometimes people do seem to try to circumvent these limitations. It doesn't happen often and never by the true professionals. Nevertheless, it occurs enough that it deserved a mention, as yes music supervisors do notice.

Please don't continue sending 5 tracks a day until you are asked to stop. Send *one* email with music and a second *only* if you find another track or two that you truly think fit the brief better than anything you've sent so far.

It's also frequently noticeable when you've thrown in "priority" tracks that are not related a search just because you know a music supervisor is paying attention. While the motivation is understandable, it's incredibly frustrating. If there is other music on your slate that you want to bring to their attention, please limit the selection and put it in a separate link within the email (e.g. "Also, I know you're buried but I'm really excited about this single/artist/album/EP so I wanted to include a link to check that out as well!")

If you don't have any tracks that fit the search parameters, that's okay! Please be honest about it. Every music supervisor I know would rather a pitching company admit to coming up empty over taking the time to go through twenty tracks that are all way off base.

4. Explain anything that may not be clear.
Perhaps you think you have a track that would be awesome for the spot...but doesn't match all requirements of the brief. Maybe the lyrics fit but the tone doesn't, or the lyrics fit but it's a male artist and the music supervisor specified female only. You have a song that was originally written in 1920 and have meticulously ensured the sound quality

matches that era...but it was recorded two years ago. Should you include it?

Your creative instincts are welcome (even appreciated) when they come from a place of true passion for a project or search. That said, strive to limit these "exceptions" to one or two songs only and be clear upfront that you are aware they aren't exactly what was requested. Then as succinctly as possible explain why you wanted to send them anyway. It's essential to demonstrate you really took the brief to heart especially if you are building a relationship with a music supervisor. Without an explanation, it's possible they will assume you simply didn't read closely enough.

Similarly, if you are including a song that has a long marching band introduction before turning into the EDM track the music supervisor requested, it doesn't hurt to point out the section they should focus on. Music supervisors do the same when sending music to editors and music editors all the time. Admittedly, I should be fully listening to all the music sent, but sometimes (often) I'm crunched for time and might only listen to the first and last fifteen seconds before moving on. Maybe the chorus is off topic, but the pre-chorus and chorus are spot on for what is happening in the scene, and the ending has a great build in the last 10 seconds. If not immediately obvious, it is in your best interest to make sure the music supervisor hears what you are hearing and understand why the song was included.

Lastly, please be upfront if a song is in serious consideration (or likely being used) for another project that will be released around the same time. Especially if it is a featured placement in a high profile project. It would be extremely frustrating if two television shows used the same end title song on the same night. While it can be extremely hard to know this information, if in doing a little research on both projects, it seems possible such a thing could happen, it's safer to note this than omit.

All of this information goes a long way to show you truly care about meeting our needs and have put thought into the music you're sending.

5. Include multiple file formats and versions.

As with general pitches, start by sending MP3s, but also consider including the option to download high-resolution versions (WAV or AIF) in a separate folder. The same applies for instrumental versions and clean versions of explicit songs. That way, if one is urgently requested by an editor or music editor, the music supervisor can get it to them ASAP.

If a music supervisor does have to reach out to you for an instrumental or WAV version (something that happens all the time), try not to respond with, "Let me reach out to the artist/producer to see if I can get." Whether you are the artist or represent them, it's to your advantage to have all of these materials at your fingertips for every song in your catalog. To not be able to turn them around within an hour or two could easily cost you a placement. That said, if a song was recorded live, analog or using another technique that prohibits an instrumental version being created, please share that when pitching. This is regularly the case with vintage tracks, so if you are pitching an older catalog it likely won't come as a shock.

6. Be as organized as possible. This is one area where music supervisors can really differ in their requirements. That said, many appreciate when the following are all in order...

- *All key metadata is embedded in the tracks sent* as described in Chapter 2, especially accurate song titles, artist and album titles, as well as company information (ideally including ownership percentages of the portion you represent as well as the other rights-holders if possible) and most importantly, your contact information.
- *Include the list of songs (with artist names) you're sending in the body of the email.* Add any notes you might also want to write to the music supervisor such as, "begin at 1:00" or, "note explicit lyrics at 45 seconds in" or, "tonally this matches the James Blake reference, but the lyric is about a sad clown preparing to end his life instead of a young girl coming of age." An exception to this is if you are asked to send a very large quantity of music. In such a situation, consider attaching an Excel spreadsheet. Regardless, it can be extremely beneficial for a

music supervisor to have an "at-a-glance" reference of song titles and artists if needed when we're on the go and need to access this information quickly. I regularly search through emails to find out who pitched certain songs or artists, and not having to click through links to find the information makes the process much faster.

- *Make sure YOUR company name is somewhere in the name of the main download folder.* This is recommended for all music sent whether it's for a specific search or not. If a music supervisor is working quickly and downloads ten folders of music at one time (which happens regularly), it's much more helpful for each folder to contain the name of the company it's coming *from* rather than their company's name or the project name only. When digging through our bloated download folders anywhere from two hours to two months later, recalling who or where that one folder came from is a difficult task. Other labels to consider including in the download folder name (if applicable): project name, fee range (e.g. $5K all in), scene and/or search name (e.g. Gritty Dive Bar, Epic Rock) and date submitted, depending on the priority indicated by the music supervisor. An example of a great download folder name would be "Pop Tart Records – Sweet Sixteen Party EDM $5K ALL IN – 5.21.17".

- *Use sub-folders.* If you're asked to send large

quantities of music, e.g. songs for multiple scenes, consider organizing into sub-folders so that no individual folder contains more than 6 - 8 songs. Individual scenes should have their own folders, but it can also be helpful to include sub-folders by fee tier ($2K all in, $5K all in, $12K all in), vocal type (male and female), tempo (down/low, mid, up) or by genre (Pop & Soul, Rap & Hip Hop, R&B).

- *Keep the email subject line as clear as possible.* Clearly indicate the project, search name and/or topic being discussed. Yes, sometimes music supervisors will be in a rush and title search emails "HELP!" or "NEED POP NOW." Instead of replying, "RE: HELP!" show off your organizational skills by re-naming your submission email to include the show and episode number (if you have) and the type of scene or content (Sorority Party, Pop Like Katy Perry, etc.) For example, "CLAWS #107 / One Stop Strip Club R&B / Awesome Publishing Inc."

7. Aim for as few clicks (and emails) as possible. As discussed in Chapter 4, never send files as attachments. Instead, use a sharing platform that allows the creation of shared links (e.g. Box). Ideally, you should only be sending *one* email, regardless of the number of scenes you're submitting music for. Copy and paste the link(s) to stream/download your playlist(s) into the email body, a function fairly intuitive in all of the services listed previously (Hightail, Box, etc.)

It's understood that company mandated platforms can make this impossible. Outside of that, the less emails and clicks to get to the music, the better.

8. Know your co-owners. As mentioned, music supervisors love when information on ownership percentages - both yours and any other rights-holders e.g. co-publishers or master recording owner - are included in a pitch. Preferably this information is included in the metadata of the track so it resides there indefinitely, but in the body of the submission e-mail works for as well. Knowing something is one-stop (or not) upfront massively speeds up our process and we'll be forever grateful.

If you really want to go the extra mile on a search, call your fellow rights-holders on a song and "pre-clear" the use with them prior to sending to the music supervisor. This may be a controversial request, but often when a fee (or fee range) specified in a search, it's expected that you have vetted any songs sent with other rights-holders prior to sending. The same applies if information about any questionable content (drug use, violence, politically or socially incendiary, etc.), previous song use denials or any other struggles is provided upfront. In these scenarios, it's better to take the time to make sure no complications will arise than rush to send tracks - even if it means you are only sending two instead of twenty options. It is not helpful to be sent a song "pre-cleared" for a low all in fee only to find out later that the publishing is with a major publisher (e.g. Sony/ATV or Warner/Chappell) and they have no knowledge of the use. If you cannot confirm that the publisher agrees to the fee, how can the song be considered pre-cleared?

Yes, I know you only represent one portion of a song. And it can be extremely difficult (and time consuming) to track the intricacies of rights-holders outside your sphere, especially if you are working with a large catalog. Music supervisors and music clearance specialists are more than comfortable making calls to the other song owners themselves. At the end of the day though, it benefits you and your clients to have relationships with those who control the rest of the song - especially if you are new to the game and trying to establish trust with a music supervisor. All music supervisors have stories of songs being pitched as "easy clear" or within a certain fee range by one rights-holder...then we put in a call to the co-publisher or master owner who laughs in our face at the very notion. The outcome of such scenarios can be that the person pitching appears out of touch with their own catalog and any music sent going forward suddenly becomes a risk.

If, for whatever reason, contacting the other rights-holders directly is simply not an option, at least be well aware of the licensing history of those tracks you only partially control. Are you turning around quotes quickly, but notice nothing ever gets to the finish line? It's possible another songwriter or rights-holder is complicating the process.

The more information you can pass along to music supervisors on potential red-flags or roadblocks early in the process, the happier we will be and the more we will trust you know what you're doing.

9. Keep it confidential. If a music search comes your way via email or phone, regardless of whether it's mentioned or not, it is *never* okay to forward it to writer or producer friends or post about it on your website or social media feeds. If at all possible, avoid blasting it out in any fashion. There have been situations where sync "agents" sent a search to their entire client list and the result was a music supervisor directly receiving music submissions from a total stranger who runs a car dealership in Chicago.

Most of the details included in music searches are confidential (budgets, scene synopses, songs that need replacing, in particular), and we could get fired if the information leaks out. Publicizing a search will quickly get you omitted from that music supervisor's list and could earn you a bad reputation throughout the industry.

If you do hear about a search you weren't included on, please don't take it personally. If I reached out to every person I knew for every search (even just the people I personally enjoy working with or whose catalogs we think are strong), I would be overwhelmed with music. If you have a relationship with the music supervisor and believe you may have songs that fit the search, give them a call or send an email inquiring whether it is okay to submit.

10. Be flexible. You put blood, sweat and tears (not to

mention money) into your music and after months of reaching out to music supervisors, you finally get a search...for little or no money. What do you do? Whether you put your music into the ring or decline to respond is ultimately up to you, and a good music supervisor will respect your choice either way. Honestly. That said, if you want to build a relationship with a music supervisor, the more flexible you can be early on, the more likely they are to come back. Most really do try to return the favor whenever they can. Maybe it is a gratis indie film use now, but that music supervisor gets a hit network television show a year or two later and comes back to you with a bigger platform and more money. Research the music supervisor. If they don't seem to have much going on, you may want to proceed with caution. If they have an extensive list of credits with projects in various stages of production, chances are they would be a good person to be in business with. Synchronization fee aside, you will still get public performance royalties (songwriter and publisher if applicable) from the music airing in television, film and some Internet channels.

Having said that, you should be very wary if a music supervisor or pitching company asks *you* to pay *them* to get a song placed. This is not the norm, and it is strongly advised against. Do your research on the person, the company and their projects before engaging in any conversation with them.

11. Don't follow up. No music supervisor likes to receive the email, "Just checking in. Did any of those tracks work?" Even worse, "I noticed you didn't download the tracks I sent. Can you please do so?" which hugely irritates almost every music supervisor. Similarly, don't be offended if your request for feedback on your pitch selections goes unanswered. While I would love to be able to offer insight, usually time simply doesn't allow.

As discussed in the previous chapter, follow-ups are understood and acceptable in certain situations. When it comes to music specifically submitted for a music search however, please trust that if any of your tracks were in strong consideration, you will be contacted.

It's usually a sign your song is still in the running if you receive a request for an instrumental or WAV version of a song (assuming you didn't include one initially) or receive a clearance or quote request. It is essential to respond to any requests that come your way as quickly as possible – especially if the music supervisor mentions an impending mix or delivery date. Once again, the "final mix" on a film or television show is when the audio elements are finalized. If you are able to send WAV versions of the vocal, instrumental and a cappella mixes along with a fully completed quote approval letter within hours after you're asked - you can bet a music supervisor want to do more business with you. On the other hand, if a clearance hurdle *does* present itself at the eleventh hour - surprise co-publisher, sample, etc. - it might be a while before another such call comes your way. Miss the mark on the creative part of a search, and a music supervisor may continue to reach out. Botching a clearance is a different story. The worst situation to be in as a music supervisor is telling a creator they can't have a song they've fallen in love with, especially if you're the one who sent it to them in the first place.

As detailed in Chapter 1, however, a clearance request does not mean your song will definitely be used. Wait until you get a confirmation letter, license or other assurance the song is locked before shouting from the rooftops...or expecting any payment.

Even if you hear nothing and another song is ultimately chosen - still have faith. Many music supervisors keep search submissions in folders or playlists for future reference. Maybe the song wasn't quite right for the teen prom scene, but a similar creative need (e.g. a sweet sixteen party) comes up a year later on a different project, and it finds its way back in consideration. This happens all the time. As with general submissions, links to music submitted for a search should never expire! If a playlist is not downloaded immediately, there is a good chance it's saved in an email inbox for future reference. I regularly go back into old searches to revisit the music sent.

I'm always on the lookout for stellar music and great collaborators who will make my professional life easier. Prove you can be that resource, and I'll come back again and again...and it's likely others will too.

6 LEVELING UP

So you've been following all the advice laid out in this book for a few months now. What happens next?

If you are an emerging label, publisher or third-party pitching company, hopefully you're on your way to forming real relationships with music supervisors. You've received a handful of searches and perhaps had a couple meeting requests come to fruition. While you may be tempted to hang your hat on these victories and press harder on those music supervisors you now know for more attention or to help expand your network – proceed with extreme discretion. As mentioned early on, the productive growth of these relationships is something you can't force. The most profitable relationships in the long term are the ones that develop organically. The best overall plan is to continue to regularly service your stellar music, and remind your contacts every so often that you are ready and willing to make their lives easier. Then, deliver on your word!

If you are an independent artist with representation, hopefully you have a greater understanding of the work being done by those pitching your music (a/k/a your "sync team") to make things happen for you. Respectively, you can ensure they have all the materials they need and that you respond to requests from them in a speedy and comprehensive nature. The more savvy and accommodating you prove yourself to be, the more those pitching your music will want to work with you and the more their music supervisor clients will want to work with your music. Once again, while great music is an essential starting point, it is those willing to collaborate that are truly memorable.

If you're an independent artist without representation, perhaps you'll land a few featured placements and companies will come calling. Awesome! As detailed in Chapter 3, music supervisors are significantly more likely to listen to music submitted (and solicit ideas) from a trusted source.

Of course, it's not as simple as saying, "YES" to the first request that comes your way.

Since I do not have any experience working for one of these companies - publishers, labels, third-party pitchers, sync agencies, etc. - I won't attempt to explain the nuances of a publishing deal or to give you a checklist of factors to consider before signing a contract. Even mentioning these subjects would be included caused some colleagues on the pitching side to exclaim, "That alone could be an entire book!" It is important however, to provide an overview of some of the arrangements that exist and how these different structures affect us as music supervisors.

Publishing Deals

With placements under your belt and a considerable catalog, companies may reach out about a publishing deal or an outright purchase of the rights to your catalog and/or future music you or your clients create. These deals vary widely. They can range from a one-time flat buyout fee to revenue splits based on negotiated percentages, can sometimes include mechanical royalties, publishing advances, etc. The important detail to note is that you are giving up your publishing rights per the requirements of the deal (i.e. for a certain amount of time, for certain songs, under certain songwriting conditions, etc.) You would keep your songwriting royalties, but not all of your publishing royalties.

Why would someone ever agree to this? If the publishing company has a wide reach internationally not only can they get your music into the hands of more music supervisors worldwide...they can track and chase down your royalties abroad as well. A good publishing company also can set you up to collaborate with other songwriters. And that's just the beginning. Ultimately though it's up to you or your clients to gauge how much control you want to give up in return for revenue or opportunity and what kind of real opportunity there is. Do your research before committing to anything.

Administration Deals

An administration deal is perhaps the most ubiquitous in the world of pitching music for media. A type of publishing deal, it consists of a third party administering or managing your catalog of music, normally for sync rights specifically, without actually owning the rights to the content. It can be for the publishing or master recording (or both) and doesn't need to be the entirety of either. It's possible for a company to administer the 10% of the publishing you control on a song. Most of the "third-party pitching companies" large and small referenced throughout this book sign artists primarily via administration deals. Often they get paid via taking a percentage out of the sync fee from whatever they place, but the fee structures can vary depending on the deal. You will still get your publishing and songwriting royalties.

Co-Publishing Deals

This is somewhat of a hybrid of the deals above where a company or individual wants to split the publishing rights to your existing catalog or future material in exchange for various services or fees. They may have access to opportunities and exposure you otherwise wouldn't and could generate income from your catalog. They'll get a percentage of the publishing rights for an upfront fee, a commission or percentage of any income they generate, or a combination of both (but once again the deals can vary in this ever changing business).

Re-Titling

This is a controversial topic. Re-titling is when a company registers one of your existing songs under a new or altered title with ASCAP, BMI or SESAC (in the United States). This is done so said company can earn performance income on uses they procure by putting this new or altered title on cue sheets associated with the procured use.

For example, a music library may want to represent your catalog for a 25% share of any sync fees they receive and a 25% cut of the publishing rights. You don't want them to receive royalties on any previous placements you've gotten on your own (including possible re-airing, syndication, etc.) By using an alternate title, the company won't earn any income not related to the uses they bring to the table.

Here is what two registrations for the same song might look like:

Original Registration
Song Title: "Party Time"
Writer: John Smith (ASCAP) 100%
Publisher: John Smith Rocks Publishing (ASCAP) 100%

Re-Registered Title
Song Title: "Party Time MUSICCO"
Writer: John Smith (ASCAP) 100%

Publisher: John Smith Rocks Publishing (ASCAP) 75% / Music Co Publishing (ASCAP) 25%

By doing this, you continue to receive all your royalties from previous placements (or radio airplay, streams or any other exploitation of your catalog) and any new activity you get with the original title name outside of the library deal. They get their 25% cut for the placements they secure with the new titles. If the deal expires or is terminated, then the re-registered title names are simply no longer used – though you and the company will continue to receive performance royalties after the expiration of the deal for uses generated by the company during the term of the deal.

This process can create an administrative burden for the PROs (who then have the same song registered in their database multiple times) and might become problematic with the rise of new technologies - digital fingerprinting, watermarking, etc. In the past, PROs would rely solely on cue sheets to discern which songs get paid royalties. As digital fingerprinting is increasingly used to track performances, the PROs will not be able to discern which registrations should be matched to which performances.

All of that said, re-titling seems to be more and more common as people in the industry continue to try to find new ways of generating income with their music.

Exclusive vs. Non-Exclusive Deals

Re-titling is one arrangement that can enable multiple companies to pitch the same catalog of songs. However, not all "non-exclusive" deals require there to be any sort of publishing rights ownership claimed.

For clarity, a "non-exclusive" deal is one wherein multiple agents or companies are pitching the same artist and/or catalog of songs. Whoever lands the placement gets the commission. "Non-exclusive" deals are, of course, appealing in that an artist has different representatives all working on their behalf, each with a slightly different range of contacts. What can happen, though, is companies will put more effort and promotion into artists and catalogs they work with exclusively. As the sole party responsible for an artist's sync career, it benefits only them to invest in their client. This is not always the case, however, so make sure to do your research before committing your catalog to one company.

From a music supervisor's perspective, it can be frustrating to get the same song pitched from multiple sources. It's then on us to decide who is credited with the pitch and respectively, which company the song is cleared and ultimately licensed through. Many music supervisors simply go by whoever sent the song first, but what if we come across multiple versions of the song in our personal song library (i.e. it was not pitched for a specific search)? To which company should the use be attributed? Some music supervisors steer clear of such tracks entirely to avoid the risk of an angry phone call claiming that a song was never cleared, when in fact it was cleared through a different party.

There is no patently right or wrong arrangement. More important than the specific deal you have with your sync agent is that you work with the agent or company you feel best meets your personal and professional needs. Choose a sync representative the same way you would any other member of your team - manager, booking agent, publicist, etc. Find someone with the relationships you're looking for, who is truly passionate about your music and who wants to be a part of your journey as an artist.

WHAT'S NEXT?

As mentioned in the Introduction, this book is a primer, not a bible. For every "common" situation, there are a handful of exceptions. You should continue to expand your knowledge of copyright law, music publishing and more. A few great resources for those interested in a comprehensive understanding of the legal components of music licensing and the business of being an artist today (and all artists should be interested) can be found on the Resources page at the end of this book.

Regardless of where you are in your career, it's important to keep in mind that landing syncs can take some time. There are many stories of artists bailing on agreements or firing sync agents because the placements didn't start rolling in immediately. Most colleagues with years of experience in the field tell their artists to give it at least a year before they can expect results, and even then, there are no guarantees. With so many artists and companies vying for attention, getting on the radar is a gradual process. There is, of course, the possibility something will happen sooner, but it's the exception rather than the rule. As always, be patient and prepared.

When you do finally land a use, make the most of it! Synchronization is just one stop on the journey to becoming a successful recording artist. It's a cog, not the whole machine. The biggest rewards will come from using all your tools in harmony. Promote the heck out of a placement on all of your social media platforms, announce to your mailing list, use the opportunity to release new content, kick off a tour...build buzz around it no matter how featured or background the use (and sometimes the uses will be in the deep, deep background). The bands that seemingly "broke" from a single use are extraordinarily rare, so treat any "sync" as a launch pad rather than the final destination. A placement on its own may not mean much, but used as a jumping off point to launch a marketing campaign - that is how having your music in media can really move the needle on a career.

7 RESOURCES

Books

All You Need to Know About the Music Business, 9th Edition by Donald S. Passman

Kohn on Music Licensing, 4th Edition by Al and Bob Kohn

The Indie Guidebook to Music Supervision for Films by Sharal Churchill

Master Music Licensing by Michael Elsner

Music Business Handbook and Career Guide by David and Tim Baskerville

Music Money and Success, 7th Edition: The Insider's Guide to Making Money in the Music Business by Jeffrey and Todd Brabec

Music Publishing - The Complete Guide by Steve Winogradsky

Music Supervision 2: The Complete Guide to Selecting Music for Movies, TV, Games and New Media by Ramsay Adams, David Hnatiuk and David Weiss

The Plain and Simple Guide to Music Publishing: What You Need to Know About Protecting and Profiting from Music Copyrights, 3rd Edition by Randall D. Wixen

Classes

Music Supervision for Film & Television at UCLA Extension

Berkeley Online Music Supervision Course

The Art of the Song Pitch

Music Licensing Bootcamp

The Access Course

Breaking Through The Noise: 4 Weeks Course

Conferences

South by Southwest (SXSW) Music Conference (Austin, TX)

Nashville Film Festival (Nashville, TN)

ASCAP I Create Music EXPO (Los Angeles, CA)

Durango Songwriters Expo (Ventura & Santa Ynez, CA and Durango, CO)

MUSEXPO (Los Angeles, CA)

Guild Of Music Supervisors State of Music in Media Conference (Los Angeles, CA)

Canadian Music Week (Toronto, ON)

Canadian Music Café at TIFF (Toronto, ON)

Sync Summit (Worldwide)

Organizations

Association of Independent Music Publishers(AIMP)

American Association of Independent Music (A2IM)

National Association of Record Industry Professionals (NARIP)

The California Copyright Conference (CCC)

The Guild of Music Supervisors

SPECIAL THANKS

The author would like to thank the following people for their invaluable help and support in the creation of this book.

Alec Sharpe, without whom this book would not have happened.

Andrew Thomas
The Krieg Family
Neophonic Music & Media
The Guild of Music Supervisors
Julia Michels
Julianne Jordan
Dave Jordan
PJ Bloom
Evyen Klean
Lenny Wohl
Tracy McKnight

SPECIAL THANKS

Russell Ziecker

Daryl Berg

Traci Larson

Peter Davis

Daniel Kuypers

Todd Porter

Jackie Shuman

Rob Lowry

Garrett McElver

Jen Malone

Stephen Stallings

Susan Dolan

Liz Lawson

Brienne Rose

Jonathan Rosner

Devon DeVries

Emily Weber

Kat Basolo

Amy Eligh

Randall Foster

Rachel Komar

Jeff Freundlich

Josh Briggs

Priya Autrey

Kristen Agee

Liz Rogers

Made in United States
North Haven, CT
23 December 2023

46467212R00093